Protective Wraps

D1655836

Protective Wraps

Transcultural aid for families

Kitlyn Tjin A Djie

Irene Zwaan

Dedicated to Ellen Meijer (1944-2020)

2021 uitgeverij koninklijke van gorcum

© 2021 Royal Van Gorcum B.V., P.O. Box 43, 9400 AA Assen, The Netherlands

All rights reserved. No part of this publication may be reproduced, stored in a retrieval system, or transmitted, in any form or by any means, electronic, mechanical, photocopying, recording, or otherwise, without the prior permission of the Publisher.

NUR 752, 753

ISBN 978 90 232 5784 4

Publisher: Uitgeverij Koninklijke Van Gorcum, Assen, the Netherlands
Cover: Renata Zincone, London (UK)
Drawing cover: Robin Fiolet (4 years old)
Drawing Sankofa: George Schriemer
Lay-out: Richard Bos
Printing: Royal Van Gorcum, Raalte, the Netherlands

Content

Foreword   9

Justification   11

Introduction   13

Reading Guide   17

1 **Kitlyn's story**   17
    Suriname   18
    Migration   19
    Family Drive   21
    Protective Wrap   23
    Finally   24
    Assignment   24

2 **Protective Wraps**   25
    Origin of 'Protective Wraps'   26
    Wat exactly is 'Protective Wraps'?   27
    Compose yourself   29
    A biological process   31
    Facilitating 'Protective Wraps'   32
    Finally   34
    Assignment   34

3 **Diverse Drenthe**   35
    Peat and sand   36
    Language   37
    Extended families   39
    Noaberschap   39
    Coexistence   40
    Working on diversity in Drenthe   41
    Superdiversity, inclusion and exclusion   42

Communitas	44
Finally	46
Assignment	46

4 The strength of families — 47

Two families thrown together	48
I-oriented systems and we-oriented systems	50
The collective we-oriented system	50
The individual I-oriented system	51
Communication styles	52
Families in the Netherlands	52
Parenting in the Netherlands	53
Single mothers	54
Attention to fathers	55
Intergenerational family thinking	56
Family continuity	57
In search of dominant views	58
Family story	58
Family as a protective system	60
Destructive family patterns	61
Finally	62
Assignment	63

5 Impact of migration — 65

Migration is a special life phase transition	67
Language	68
Effect of migration on family continuity	69
Different generations	71
Commuting	73
Affronts	73
Protective wraps in the transitional space	75
The best of both worlds	76
Finally	77
Assignment	77

6 Intercultural competencies — 79

Knowledge of your own cultural baggage	80
Knowing the Other	83
Sacred cows	83
Switching perspectives	84
Hidden dimensions	86
Communicating with compassion and empathy	87
Finally	90
Assignment	90

7 Instruments for the intercultural dialogue — 91
Genograms — 92
Contextual questions — 97
The lifeline — 98
TOPOI — 99
Combining TOPOI with genograms — 102
Life story — 102
Testimony — 104
Finally — 106
Assignment — 106

8 New perspective in care — 107
All the elements of the model in a row — 108
What distinguishes 'Protective wraps'? — 110
Dominant discourse — 110
The relationship — 111
Continuity — 112
Unorthodox solutions — 114
How does 'Protective wraps' relate to regular approaches in care? — 115
How does 'Protective wraps' relate to the requirements of new style welfare? — 117
The organization as 'Protective wrap' — 120
Sankofa — 120
Assignment — 121

Word of thanks — 122

About the authors — 124

Literature — 125

Foreword

In 2016 it's once again time for a revised edition. I am glad that this book continues to be a great and lasting source of inspiration for anyone committed to working in the care sector in an honest and non-judgmental way.

The book is the result of a project of Bureau Jeugdzorg Drenthe (youth care agency in the province of Drenthe). All its employees have with great dedication been working on carrying out a special assignment, which in actual fact should not be 'special', but should be normal and continuous: providing truly accessible and well-functioning care for all parents and children in Drenthe, including those who are migrants or Dutch with migrant backgrounds.

As a project team, we knew that quite a lot had been written already about transcultural work. However, we wanted to augment the range of publications with one based on practice and focused on the core of transcultural work for care workers themselves.

In the context of the transcultural work project, Kitlyn Tjin A Djie has trained many workers, both within Bureau Jeugdzorg Drenthe and at our chain partners. The province of Drenthe has been of great support in putting the diversity policy issue high on the agenda.

During the training sessions, the tremendous amount of personal knowledge and experience of case managers, family guardians and care workers became apparent. In their unconscious form, personal experiences sometimes turn out to create barriers in contacts with others. Once brought to light, however, these personal life experiences of course also prove to be the very source for establishing real contact, on a human level and irrespective of belief, history or race.

How to tap into this source, that's what this book is essentially about. This means that it is not a technical treatise on models and methods. It is about knowing and acknowledging your own history, and on that basis dispensing with preconceived ideas and seeking real dialogue with the other person. Even in stressful and hazardous situations.

At a time when imposing norms on 'foreigners' seems to occupy a fairly central position, this choice is as brave as it is necessary. To add to this, I believe that the core of intercultural work is in fact perfectly organically connected to the solution-oriented and systemic approach, to which we have been committed for years in youth care in Drenthe.

I would sincerely like to thank Irene Zwaan and Kitlyn Tjin A Djie for having written this book and in doing so having made the power of protective wraps accessible to professionals throughout the country. I would equally like to thank all our people who have contributed and who have made their stories available in order to share their experiences with their colleagues now and in the future.

Cees Wierda
Director Bureau Jeugdzorg Drenthe

This book was written as part of the more comprehensive transcultural relief project, in which attention was paid to improving the connection between professional care and existing (family) cultures.

Justification

This book reflects the views of Kitlyn Tjin A Djie on how to bring out the best in children, particularly migrant children, in youth care. Her philosophy is based on her own life story and her experiences. She supports her ideas with theoretical concepts from anthropology, intercultural communication and system therapy.

Kitlyn uses her own story and the stories of others to substantiate her ideas. In the anthropological and social sciences, the use of personal stories to underpin certain beliefs is also known as the narrative approach. The principle of the narrative approach is that in the stories of people and in the language they use to tell these stories, certain ideas relating to a theme are expressed. Stories illustrate the complexity and diversity of ideas and realities. The narrative method gives people a voice; it ascribes value to the story. It gives meaning to the knowledge of those concerned and places this knowledge in the light of a greater whole.[1] There are numerous ways of presenting and analyzing narratives. There are no real formal rules. You cannot be objective in using narratives in order to substantiate theories. What you can do is draw plausible conclusions if a number of stories point in the same direction. The stories in this book bridge the gap between theory and practice. Kitlyn's own life story led to certain views. She looked for the theory to corroborate these. This theory is subsequently illustrated with stories from third parties.

This book presents the ideas and beliefs of Kitlyn Tjin A Djie. It does not always provide a platform for nuance. And because her views are so interwoven with her own story and experiences, she herself is also prominently present in the chapters.

No ready-made blueprint or prefab solutions are provided in this book. It is intended to offer a new perspective on reality, different from the one you have been accustomed to up till now. This might just raise more questions than it provides answers, but it will certainly make you think. And hopefully it will help you put those case studies where initially you could see no way out in a different perspective, enabling you to give a new direction to solutions.

Most of the stories in this book were told by Kitlyn and by employees of Bureau Jeugdzorg Drenthe. Aspects in the stories that might lead to recognizability such as names, place names, problems and country of origin of clients have in most cases been altered.

---

1 Does, M. van den en A. Arce (1998), 'The value of narratives in rural development projects. A case from Equador', *Journal of agricultural education and extension*, vol. 5, nr. 2, pp. 85-98.

Introduction

This is a book about Kitlyn Tjin A Djie, transcultural system therapist. Kitlyn uses her own story, her family history, in order to show why intergenerational family thinking is so important in the provision of care. And how collective family systems function. Kitlyn's story is about diversity, migration and moving back and forth between contexts and cultures. She herself is a migrant from Suriname (former Dutch colony) with Chinese, Vietnamese, Portuguese, Creole and German blood. She originates from Jewish, Catholic and Protestant traditions. Her father stemmed from a patriarchal system, her mother from a matriarchal one. To this day, her family lives all over the world. If there is one person who knows what she's talking about on the subject of diversity, it's Kitlyn. Kitlyn is married to a Dutchman. She has two adult sons and seven grandchildren. She knows better than anyone that it takes certain skills to keep the door open for dialogue with 'the Other'[2]. She calls attention to the consequences of migration. She offers tools for the care worker to contribute to the welfare of those who have lost their way as a result of a life phase transition such as migration. To achieve this, it is essential to switch between cultures, to look at things from different angles and to set aside sacred cows. In order to be able to do that, some knowledge about the other person is required, such as culture, family structure, traditions. But more than that, care workers must be aware of their own cultural stock-in-trade. They must be able to deploy a personally vulnerable part of themselves to allow for genuine contact with the client. Different strategies and methodologies can be of assistance in this respect. It is important to look for protective wraps for the client. 'Protective Wraps' is a term for providing protection by wrapping someone in familiar circumstances. Rituals, photographs, bringing back experiences from the past, creating situations to offer some safety and warmth in a difficult phase of someone's life.

    This is also a book about the province of Drenthe, with its very diverse social landscape. There are many rural areas and relatively few cities. There is a peat culture and a sand culture. There is the history with the Moluccans (inhabitants former Dutch colony), the train hijacking (see chapter 3). Drenthe has its own traditions, its 'noaberschap' (the unwritten rule to always help your neighbors), the villages with greens surrounded by farms, but also the dolmens, the war, the secrets, the poverty. In Drenthe, different dialects are associated with different cultures.

---

2   Levinas, E (English 1969) *Totality and Infinity: An Essay on Exteriority*. Pittsburgh: Duquesne University Press.

Drenthe is beautiful, Drenthe is wide and complex. Drenthe offers an attractive environment that illustrates how an original Dutch culture can carry diversity within it, and how the different Dutch cultures can interact. It is also revealed how it relates to the consequences of immigration. In this book, Drenthe represents a small part of the Netherlands. Because each province has its own history and cultural characteristics.

Bureau Jeugdzorg Drenthe wants to be accessible to all young people. That is why in 2005 a diversity project was launched, in which Kitlyn partook. At the time, she trained all Bureau Jeugdzorg Drenthe employees in transcultural communication. As a result, they were better equipped to deal with clients who 'speak a different language' from that of the care worker. Her trainings were like a warm bath. Without tools or programs, she lures participants into a kind of extended personal conversation, during which everyone tells fascinating stories. As one of them put it: "Alignment with the family stories of the other participants is the best teacher. To be aware of your own cultural heritage makes you a good care worker." Bureau Jeugdzorg Drenthe had positive experiences with Kitlyn's philosophy and working method. That is why in 2006, Irene Zwaan and Kitlyn Tjin A Djie were asked to write this book, of which the first edition appeared in 2007.

In addition to Kitlyn's stories and theories, the experiences and stories of the employees of Bureau Jeugdzorg Drenthe are recorded in this book. In Drenthe it is demonstrated that the intercultural dialogue not only applies to migrants. Wherever there are differences, wherever there is diversity in the broadest sense of the word, attention should be given to intercultural communication. This includes the communication between men and women, young and old, protestant and catholic, employer and employee, care worker and client; in short, this way of thinking is valuable in all forms of communication.

This book can be read as a novel, a storybook. In her work with migrants, Kitlyn started off with her own story, her intuition and experiences. She was convinced that in order to help children who end up in the care sector, white Dutch mindsets don't work. Subsequently, she found the accompanying theory. This book, too, starts off with the story. The story of Kitlyn and the stories of Bureau Jeugdzorg Drenthe employees. Together, the stories paint a model. 'Protective Wraps' is a model in which different theoretical concepts provide tools for shaping the dialogue with the unknown stranger in an honest and human way.

Addition to the 4th revised edition

The Dutch version of *Protective Wraps, transcultural aid for families* was born in Drenthe, after which it took off and landed in various places throughout the country. There have been a number of developments, some of which are worth mentioning here.

An important impulse, for example, was that at the presentation of the book in Assen, capital of the province of Drenthe, several organizations joined forces to establish the platform Protective Wraps in Drenthe. This platform, consisting of organizations for education, care and welfare work, has made an important contribution to the distribution of Protective Wraps in the rest of the Netherlands.

Supported by a European grant, an implementation study was carried out at seven organizations in the western part of the country, with very positive results. As a foundation for this study, PIONN (management consultancy) has developed and defined a scientific substantiation for the working model of protective wraps, which can be found on the website.

The protective wraps model is taught as a social studies subject in higher professional education. Various organizations across the country are trained in working with protective wraps.

The province of Utrecht has deployed protective wraps at eight youth care institutions, with a view to lowering thresholds for migrant children and their families. Research conducted by Forum into the impact of the project showed that there was a high appreciation for protective wraps among the participants in the training courses. The cultural sensitivity of care workers turned out to have increased significantly.

Gradually, we started putting up a house around our work: Bureau Beschermjassen (Protective Wraps Agency). Through this agency we offer training courses: basic trainings for beginners as well as trainings for those who want to teach the model to others. Kitlyn also gives lectures, workshops and in-company trainings throughout the country, meant for everyone who wants to create scope for diversity at work.

From time to time we receive comments on the fact that the book is focused too much on migrants. In such cases we argue that there is very little literature to be found on the influence of migration on family continuity in we-oriented systems, and that this book fills the gap. We also receive many positive signals regarding the major role played in the book by the provincial context of Drenthe. After all, many care providers working in cities in the northwestern Netherlands themselves have roots in the provinces of Zeeland, Limburg, Groningen or Friesland.

The protective wraps model contains a number of theoretical as well as practical elements. Everyone, regardless of personal or professional background, can make use of it. Apart from care workers, the participants at the training sessions include police officers, theater makers, midwives, civil servants and university college teachers. It's all about safety at the workplace, knowing your history, doing justice to yourself and establishing relationships with others based on your contact with yourself. No fixed methodology is entailed; everyone can set to work with it right away. At the same time, this occasionally makes it difficult to generate exposure. Databases for effective interventions, subsidizers and governments require SMART descriptions. The protective wraps model does not easily fit into such a demarcated frame. Which is precisely the strength of the model.

Addition to the 5th revised edition

The transition in youth care has led to all kinds of district teams and low-threshold facilities, where boundaries that previously existed between disciplines and organizations are less pronounced, and professionals reinforce each other instead of following separate tracks.

In 2015, Kitlyn was commissioned by the municipality of Amsterdam and Amsterdam University of Applied Sciences to provide Protective Wraps training courses to all the *Samen Doen* teams (secondary care teams for the support of families with complex problems) in the city. As usual, there were eye-openers, in particular with regard to the influence on both the professional and the client of family, history and culture over several generations. And when the entire team looked at one particular case with the aid of a genogram and lifeline, they were pleasantly surprised to note their collective knowledge and the added value of looking at case histories in that way. It became clear, for example, that the root of the problem was not a no-good child, but a family with a history of loss and ruptures, causing one parent to suffer from depressions, the other taking refuge in alcohol and the elder brother developing a gambling addiction. All those individual problems have a joint source, which is anchored in history. So it pays for all of us together to look at the one case. The participants in the training virtually always returned home cheerfully: "From now on we will see things in a different light and ask different questions!"

On balance, almost ten years after the first edition, we can conclude that the protective wraps model increasingly fits in with the framework of today's society, in which the government is focusing more and more on citizen participation and individual strength. However, the fact that an entire family history is involved remains a blind spot, both in case histories and in your conduct as a professional. This means that we will continue our mission with a great deal of passion and conviction, and that we have much pleasure in presenting this revised 5th edition to the world.

Reading Guide

Chapter 1: Kitlyn's story

Kitlyn tells her life story. She talks about her experiences in Suriname, her migration, and the issues she comes across as a Surinamese in the Netherlands. Her personal and professional findings have resulted in 'Protective Wraps'. The ingredients in this book can all be traced back to her story as told in this chapter.

Chapter 2: Protective Wraps

This chapter is about 'Protective Wraps'. By means of the protective wraps model, people who are in an important life phase transition, as is the case with most of the clients in youth care, are embedded in the group or culture. Looking for anchors, pillars of support, rituals or equivalents from the past helps people to compose themselves and to resume their lives.

Chapter 3: Diverse Drenthe

This chapter is about the social, cultural and historic landscape of Drenthe. Experiences of care workers in Drenthe show the extent to which 'Protective Wraps' achieves alignment in the province. By zooming in on Drenthe, it is made visible how one small part of the Netherlands itself contains diversity and how 'the Other' is dealt with here. You also receive tools to help you unravel diversity in different contexts.

Chapter 4: The power of families

Families have a self-healing capacity. Because this frequently is a blind spot for care workers, attention is paid to how families function, making a distinction between family systems directed towards the individual, such as those in the Netherlands, and the more collectively oriented family systems of non-Western migrants.

Chapter 5: Impact of migration

Migration has a major impact on people from collective systems, partly because it affects the continuity of the functioning of the extended family. Herein lies a large part of the causes of problems in families. This chapter provides an insight into the consequences of migration, so that as a care worker you can take this into account.

Chapter 6: Intercultural competencies

This chapter provides an overview of the intercultural competencies required for an open dialogue with 'the Other'. This involves knowledge of your own cultural baggage and that of the other person. You should be aware of your sacred cows in order to be able to keep switching perspectives. Empathy and compassion are basic requirements in intercultural communication. Finally, you should be aware of the fact that there are always blind spots in communication.

Chapter 7: Tools for intercultural dialogue

A number of tools are discussed that can be used in the contact between the care worker and the client. Subjects addressed are working with genograms, making a visual overview of the history and structure of an extended family. The lifeline helps to get an idea of important life phase transitions. Attention will be paid to TOPOI, an analysis model for communication. Working with contextual questions, life stories and testimonials will also be discussed.

Chapter 8: New perspective on the provision of care

'Protective Wraps' offers a new perspective on the care practice. This chapter examines how it relates to conventional views on the provision of care. It also describes how it fits in with existing methodologies such as Signs of Safety, the Solution Focused Approach and the Family Network Consultation. In addition, we will discuss how it relates to the beacons of New Style Welfare.

1

Kitlyn's story

Kitlyn Tjin A Djie understands the art of breathing life into theoretical concepts. She does this by examining her own life story like an anthropologist. In this way she invites others to discover their own story. To look at the history and structure of their own family. Because their own story provides them with tools in the dialogue with the Other.

"I like to start off stories at the beginning. Where my cradle once stood. Or where my name comes from. Getting rooted, as it were. My name Kitlyn comes from the Chinese word Kit-ling. Kit-ling in Chinese means 'enough'. By the time I was born, my father reckoned that there were enough daughters. I was the fourth in a row of six girls. The fact that my father changed Kit-ling to Kitlyn leads me to point out that he is a second-generation migrant child. He has experienced the pain of loss of the first generation of migrants. But he has not personally experienced that loss. He wanted to give me a Western name. By calling me Kitlyn, he connected the West with the East, Lynn being an American name. Explaining this provides an opportunity to look behind the story. It makes me feel supported by my family. It is universal, everyone is part of a family, whether they like it or not. Talking about my family makes people find their way to their own family.

My father was Chinese, stemming from a patriarchal system. In 1866, his grandfather migrated from Themsemwui in Southeast China to Suriname. My paternal grandfather married a Vietnamese woman, born in French Guiana. She introduced the French élan. My mother is Surinamese, stemming from a matriarchal system. Her father was Portuguese-German. Her mother had a Creole father, who was a direct descendant of the enslaved. Her mother's mother was from the indigenous Caribbean tribe.

Suriname

I grew up in a privileged environment. I lived in a district of Paramaribo of which everyone said: 'I wished I could live there.' In a beautiful house, the top part made of wood and the lower part made of stone. It was very striking, with trees leaning forward under the weight of orange flowers. It was a safe nest, a dream house. My father was a white-collar worker. Initially he worked as a station manager for a North American airline. Subsequently he worked for a Dutch company. Rock Hudson and other movie stars came by to visit us. During stopovers, they had to be entertained for the day, with a festive lunch prepared by my mother. Together with people from the district, my father built a swimming pool where only posh people came to swim. My mother's closet was full of cocktail dresses and evening robes. I remember my parents as each other's partners rather than as parents. Sometimes my father got home with my mother in his arms. The two of them were always interacting with each other. One of the girls from our neighborhood remembered how mad about each other my parents were, while her father was always cheating on her mother. 'I wished I had a father like yours, a father who adored my mother!' she said.

I was a headstrong child. My mother always says that I was the weirdest child she had. I had such a quick temper! I have pushed my sisters out of the window. I was crazy about my father. He was a big friend rather than a father. He told stories about Pete Puff, a little boy who would let out a big stinky puff when danger threatened. That's how he chased away danger. But my mother was more reserved. She had to be strict, because my father wasn't.

I remember very well that as a child I felt I had special gifts in communicating. At a very young age – and I knew I was different in that respect – I was able to have a conversation with my father about the domination of the Dutch in his company. About the fact that the Dutch always took precedence over the Surinamese. And how unfair he thought that was. I was about ten years old at the time. I was one of the few children who got along well with the maids, of whom we had a whole bunch. I loved listening to them. I was fascinated by their stories about shamans in the forest. These stories were not allowed to be told or heard in our house, because they were primitive. As a six-year-old girl, I was at the needlewoman's feet, listening breathlessly to her stories from everyday life. She was a single mother with two children. And we also had an ironing lady, with whom I had frequent quarrels. My uniform always ended up being too stiff, because she used too much starch. This made me furious. Time and again I had told her: It shouldn't be stiff! What the gardener said I could never understand. With him I found comfort after I'd had one of my fits of rage. At such times I would get so angry that I had to lie down on my bed to kick it off. I was literally kicking. And when I had exhausted myself, I went to the gardener to yell at him in Dutch, which he didn't understand. But after I had finished screaming, he took my hand, comforted me, and shared his invariably peppery lunch with me. To this day, spicy food has a calming effect on me.

The oppressive atmosphere in Suriname was driving me crazy. I really very much looked forward to leaving. That environment in which you were constantly dictated how to move, how to act. Perhaps it had something to do with the midway position I occupied in the row of sisters. Three sisters were older than me, with a four years' age difference between myself and the youngest of them. There was an age difference of almost three years between the other sisters. The eldest sister had her own friends, the second and third were like two peas in a pod, always together. And then there were those two little brats that were younger than me and never did what I wanted them to do. I didn't belong anywhere. Not with the big ones and not with the little ones. My youngest sister only recently said: 'Kit, you shouldn't let your hair grow long. It makes you look much too sweet. You're not, you're a bitch, you should cut your hair.' It's funny how they keep you in your place.

Migration

We all went to study in the Netherlands. My mother was never allowed to attend teacher training college. She had to start work at fifteen. Due to the death of her father that year, poverty suddenly struck. Whereas she had wanted to become a teacher. My father had to stop studying medicine. As an undergraduate he could stay in Suriname, but to continue his studies he had to go to the Netherlands. His brother had already been in the Netherlands and had died there of tuberculosis. His eleven-year-old sister had been sent to the Netherlands by boat to receive treatment for rickets. She died on the way there. It was then that my grandfather said: 'No one will be going to the Netherlands from now on, because you will die.' As a consequence, my father was unable to complete his studies. That was the reason why my parents sent all their six daughters away. 'Be what you want to be, grab your chances.' In 1969 I left for the Netherlands. I stayed at the same house where my three elder sisters had stayed. Mr. and Mrs. Morren had had girls staying at their house from 1952 onwards. She was German, he a Dutchman, married in 1936. He was the municipal secretary in Amsterdam. I arrived in turbulent times. Mr. Morren frequently got home smelling of stink bombs. In those days, I often sat in Dam Square. I liked the feeling of nobody knowing me, of being able to revel in anonymity. To be in hiding in the years to come, that was my aim. I spent three years in that house: the fourth, fifth and sixth year of the HBS secondary school. It was a golden time. I started to enjoy learning again. I had never liked learning before. I had been living in fear under the nuns' regime. Those nuns hit you left, right and center whenever the mood took them. But here school was great. The teachers smoked joints with you. But I never lost control, always knew my limits. I thought, without my parents here, who is there to save me? So I sat there in Dam Square being a good girl.

After secondary school, I enrolled at what is these days called Social Pedagogical Care training. I didn't understand that training. I just couldn't understand the fact that the Dutch look at children without taking their context, their family, into account. I went to look for an internship that I could understand. De Triangel, where they took in entire families. Very progressive. That's where the foundation was laid for my current work with family systems. They went as far there as taking in three generations. There was a grandmother, a daughter, and a grandchild. All three of them drinking heavily. The two-year-old child poured the jenever from the teapot. And grandpa regularly paid a visit with his cane to beat everyone up. My colleague wanted to free the women from that man, and arranged for them to receive benefits. But I knew even then that these kinds of systems have been going on for centuries. It would only cause disruption to take action against that man. It would not solve the problem.

An important event around that time took place in southern Morocco. It was 1977, I was 24 years old. I got into a situation I did not recognize and in which I was unable to make clear to anyone what I needed. I was traveling with Hans, now my husband. We were in a jeep with a tour group and crashed into a military truck. The wife of a couple the same age as we were, was killed when the jeep turned over and she ended up underneath. The fact that the jeep turned over was my salvation. Initially the woman was still alive. Both of us were dragged into a van parked by the side of the road. She died on the way, a few hours later. For years I have been asking myself why it was me who had to stay alive. Seriously injured, I spent two weeks in hospital. I couldn't explain anything, and I couldn't understand what was happening. I was in much pain, but there were no medicines. I saw all kinds of men at my bed, dozens of them. They spoke Arabic, Berber, or French. Everything I needed or tried to explain failed to be understood. In their world, people who were dying were important. I only had a few broken bones. They lived in a reality totally different from mine. And the surgeon, always bare-chested and wearing an apron with blood dripping from it, was not a man whom I thought I wanted to listen to. No help was forthcoming from the Netherlands, because the owner of the jeep didn't want anybody to know about the accident. Just before, he had been involved with a death in Greenland. So he never contacted the embassy. Only two weeks later I was picked up and transported back to the Netherlands.

Meanwhile, I started my own family. I married Hans and got two sons, Robin and Michel. The hair of Michel, the youngest, started to get curly around the age of twelve. His sleek black hair turned into a full head of curls. I was delighted: It was grandma's hair, my mother's mother! But my son was appalled: 'I look like a Turk now instead of like a Dutch or Surinamese.' And my mother was stunned: 'He's got the Creoles' bad hair.' For me his hair tied him to his roots, his Creole-Portuguese great-grandmother. He had never known her. When she died he was eight years old and had never been to Suriname. What followed was a difficult year for him and for us. Friends no longer wanted to be associated with him because he looked like a Turk. He started shaving his head, and when the curly hair came back he did it again. Later he took to wearing a cap 24 hours a day. After a year of worry, we decided to visit Suriname with him. Words almost fail to describe the change that took place in him within three minutes after arrival at the airport. Peace settled over him. He looked around him, and you could almost literally see him descend into his unknown roots. Back in the Netherlands, he could feel like someone from Amsterdam again, the tension was gone. Commuting between cultures had become part of his life.[1]

Family Drive

After De Triangel I started work on a Ministry of Justice project aimed at promoting integration in children's homes. The teams didn't want any black people because they didn't look like them. While at that time, 1983, already as many as 40% of the children in that home had migrant backgrounds. I could literally see the desperation of black children there. And the disqualification of the group workers regarding the families. That made my sense of mission come to life. All who worked there were white, except for the mop lady. The mentors believed the children should decide for themselves what time they got home. They had to learn to make choices. Those children went crazy. Some of them went lying down in the middle of the highway. There was this gap between their own home and the children's home. When parents or relatives came and brought food, they were turned away. It's not visiting time, they were told. Due to my family drive we started to set up groups in which group leaders, parents and children exchanged ideas about upbringing and had meals together. It was revolutionary. The remedial educationalist I worked with totally agreed. We only disagreed on the way in which to approach migrant parents. I had no language for this, so I started looking for literature to go with what I observed, how systems work. In 1988 I was fired because I was too critical. For six years following this, I worked at a consultancy firm for young people and parents. I was given a special position and could never be fired. After a year I asked them to lift this provision because it drove me crazy. I'm not very positive about positive discrimination. Working for that consultancy firm, I learned to be attractive. We had

---

1 Previously published in Tjin A Djie, K. (2002), 'De bijzondere opdracht van migrantenkinderen'. In: C.J.A. Roosen, A. Savenije, A. Kolman en R. Beunderman (eds.) 'Over een grens', *Psychotherapie met adolescenten*, Assen: Koninklijke Van Gorcum.

to make sure that we were client-friendly, so that people would want to come back. I loved it. Every little talk, telephone call, handing out flyers. This is what youth care should be about, always giving your very best for the children, parents, and family. The coordinator brought me in with the idea that we should start interculturalizing and that 50% of the agency should become black. And that's all been realized.

During that period, based on my experiences in the children's home, I participated in methodology development for Amsterdam University of Applied Sciences (HvA). I also did a lot of teaching and started using my family as material. I learned to be attractive to my students. I taught policemen, who put all the racism that existed throughout the Netherlands on my plate. I discovered that it is an extremely complicated field to be active in. That's when I started to use the genogram, a kind of family drawing through which to demonstrate, on the basis of my own family, how migrant families 'do things'. I followed the advanced course and wrote a thesis on placing children in their own family, the so-called family placements. I had a number of colleagues in mind for whom the thesis was intended. One of them was Jannie, a very big Dutch woman. She would say: 'And then I set such a very easy target for this Surinamese mother and then she doesn't even meet it!' In other words, those people were in the first place supposed to meet *her* targets, really dreadful. I wrote a plea for putting the control of the family placements in the hands of the families themselves, not in our hands. When it comes to placements with foreign foster families, the social worker has a coordinating role. But when placing children with the family, we should take a different position. Up till then we had positioned ourselves as the ones who knew it all and were in control. So we kept losing families.

In families like mine, every generation has people who represent authority. In our case, these are my eldest sister and myself. My eldest sister had it delegated to her. I earned it because of my problem-solving ability. For example when my niece, daughter of my youngest sister, had blood poisoning. She was in a bad way, in the intensive care unit of a regional hospital. My mother, my eldest sister and I went to speak to the doctor to request a transfer to an academic hospital. The doctor said: 'What can I do with a grandmother and two aunts? Where is the mother?' To which I said: 'Why the mother? We are the ones who take the decisions.' In such a situation it is perfectly clear who does what. My eldest sister will take care of the family, another sister will stay with my youngest sister all the time, I will speak to the doctors. It is clear to the entire family how to deal with authority and with the various tasks.

I adopted Nel Jessurun as my intellectual mother. In 1989, I read an article by her about genograms. She was part of a progressive system think tank. Through her I came into contact with many hotshots and theories in the field of system therapy. In 1993, Nel Jessurun and Anke Savenije founded the Transcultural System Therapy training in response to Dutch white thinking in system therapy. In 1997 I followed that training. At college I also found a large amount of knowledge and literature. I was able to connect the things I discovered in my own family with collective system elements. I taught family guardians, social workers and foster carers all over the place. And there were always loads of new articles. And yet, I always had the feeling that the available literature was no good, was too Western. For me looking at families, generational thinking, is essential. As opposed to system thinking. System thinking is about problems that arise in the interaction with the context. In system thinking that context always consists of the father, the mother, and the child. But how do migrant families manage? Who are the figures of authority? How are decisions made? This is essential in collective systems. For me this was so obvious, I couldn't understand that my ideas were not getting across. I didn't realize that there was a blind spot there, because of that obviousness.

Protective Wrap

In the 1990s, a hotshot in the field of system therapy visited the Netherlands. She had a theory about putting a stop to violence in partner relationships. Nel Jessurun had been invited and said: 'That lady is going to tell a Western story, so I will be taking along as many black people as possible.' We went there with a number of women. It soon became apparent that the lady had no answer to our questions, nor did these questions interest her. If black people had problems within their relationships, they should seek advice in their own black community. Virtually all those present were white, and acting like: 'Oh God, there's those blacks again.' This is how our Collective Transcultural Therapists (CTT) was born, with feminists from the system therapy world. A group of women who supported and reinforced each other on their ideological and intellectual path. The collective was sacred to me. It functioned like a protective wrap. All of us taught, each one of us conveyed a controversial message at lectures. We nibbled away at the established order. People got annoyed when they heard us. We were a threat to fossilized beliefs. That's why we were so important as a collective. It was an envelope from which you could say everything you like. We were very good at inclusion and exclusion, which is really what it's all about. We all had our fight, but we were brilliant in the field of re-embedment. I was a member of CTT until 2017.

The idea of protective wraps had emerged in the early days at De Triangel. Something happened there which I regard as the key event in my entire career. At the time, in 1981, I was pregnant with my oldest son Robin. I had to tear a mentally ill mother away from her child. It was dreadful. And there the idea arose, without me having words for it, that everyone needs protective wraps. For example, when I was working in day care there was this mother from Nigeria. She had been a stewardess and married to an Antillean who abused her. She had two small sons. She didn't know anyone. She said: 'You have become my family.' But that wasn't allowed. Things had to remain separated professionally. I said what nonsense, this woman needs a temporary protective wrap. We remind her of her family, so we are going to celebrate her child's birthday. And everyone she knows is welcome! We will do it her way. Once you allow such mothers to do what they liked to do in the past, they will regain their strength. Later, I discovered the book *An olive tree on the iceberg* by Django Sterman[2], in which these ideas are presented. That provided me with the language and theory to go with my views, so I could put them into words, spread the message.

In 1995 I started my own agency. At that time, I discovered that I liked working with small groups. It enlightened me. And at the School for Coaching, where I worked from 2001 onwards, I learned how to be grand while still being humble. How to facilitate a group to realize its own goals. How to stay close as a safe big mother, but at the same time allow people to map out their own path. In other words, how to create a safe space and still remain the teacher.

Now there is Bureau Beschermjassen. I give basic training sessions and also train the trainers for everyone who wants to start working with the model in the workplace. The working model Protective Wraps is described and made accessible in this book and in a scientific description. Because I would like the philosophy and the working method to be spread freely, there is no copyright on protective wraps. In my training sessions, all of us become people who are interested in each other's life stories. Within ten minutes a sense of safety is felt, and we all want to learn from each other's life experience.

The stories in this book were told mainly during training sessions with employees of Bureau Jeugdzorg Drenthe. Their stories and mine bring the theory to life and illustrate how you can use your own story to better understand the Other."

Finally

This chapter has told Kitlyn's story. Her story contains all the elements that will be discussed further in this book. Her story is the basis for the Protective Wraps model. What is a protective wrap, what is its function, and how can you as a care worker use protective wraps to help your client? This will be comprehensively addressed in the next chapter.

Assignment

- What do you recognize in Kitlyn's story, and in what sense does it correspond to yours?
- What is totally different in her story?
- What made you think twice? In other words: what do you think is strange, or what do you disagree with?
- In what sense do you recognize aspects from her story in other people's stories, such as clients or fellow students?

---

2   Sterman, D. (1996), *Een olijfboom op de ijsberg. Een transcultureel-psychiatrische visie op en behandeling van jonge Noord-Afrikanen en hun families.* Nederlands Centrum Buitenlanders; republished by Pharos (2007).

2

Protective Wraps

Irene: "In between sessions, Kitlyn and I walked through Amsterdam looking for food (Thai, Italian, salmon, salads, chocolate, biscuits, nuts) in which to wrap ourselves while working on this book. It was too early in the year to be so warm. 'Great, this climate change!' Kitlyn said. 'Not for me, I love our seasons', I said. 'When I was living in Tanzania, I sometimes walked around naked with the air conditioner at full swing. Then, when I was freezing cold, I took a warm bath.' 'You know what that is?' Kitlyn said. 'That's protective wraps.'"

"In cultures with the 'extended family' pattern, a girl in puberty who should be informed about things like menstruation and pregnancy, can familiarize herself with such matters because adult women around her will see to it that she is prepared, and will provide explanations. Moving into a new phase, with the accompanying fears, takes place within the protective enwrapment of the group. This protection is comparable to the function of the skin in the exchange of the inner world and the outer world. For this protective enwrapment, French transcultural psychology uses the beautiful term *enveloppement*."[1] When Kitlyn read these words in the book *An olive tree on the iceberg* by Django Sterman, everything fell into place. Sterman provided a theoretical framework for the core of her ideas. Soon enough the term 'Protective Wraps' was born. In 1997, it was first published in an interview with Kitlyn in the journal Vrouw en Gezondheidszorg (Woman and Healthcare). Quote: "Everyone needs protective wraps in order to function at optimum level. Migrants must create a new support framework, because the old protective wraps have disappeared. I myself do it as well. Such a support framework often closely resembles the family or social environment of home. For the care sector it is important to take this into account."[2]

This chapter is about 'Protective Wraps', the core of Kitlyn's thinking. We will elaborate on the origin of the concept and its meaning. It will also be explained how it works, and how as a care worker you can help to apply 'protective wraps'.

Origin of 'Protective Wraps'

The origin of 'Protective Wraps' can be traced back to working with the genogram: a visual overview of an extended family. In chapter 7 we will discuss this tool in detail.

Kitlyn once drew a genogram with a Surinamese grandmother. She wanted to look for pillars of support, because the grandmother had to take care of her granddaughter all by herself, which was very hard work. As she worked on the genogram, the look in her eyes changed, as if a film had started to run. "Grandma, tell me what you see", Kitlyn said, while the grandmother was staring at all those little circles, squares and lines. She said: "I see the almond tree that I used to sit under as a child. Now I think, what should I do to make me feel good again like that, just for a little while? Perhaps I should spend some time barefoot in a sandpit." So, the genogram triggered images. Something happened, something started to flow.

Another example that made Kitlyn discover the effect of 'Protective Wraps' was in her work with a 16-year-old Moroccan girl who was pregnant. Since she had nowhere else to go, she was taken care of in the teenage mothers' home where Kitlyn worked. From the age of ten she had lived in all kinds of homes, so she had been separated from her own cultural context for a long time. She had a Moroccan boyfriend, also about 16 years old.

---

1   Sterman, D. (1996), *Een olijfboom op de ijsberg. Een transcultureel-psychiatrische visie op en behandeling van jonge Noord-Afrikanen en hun families*. Nederlands Centrum Buitenlanders; republished by Pharos (2007).
2   Bakker, H., 'Iedereen heeft beschermjassen nodig', interview with K. Tjin A Djie in *Vrouw en Gezondheid*, November/December 1997.

Kitlyn:

> *I really had the idea she was as deaf as a post. She never heard what we said, she never listened. When I said she had to go visit the midwife, she just didn't do it. But as soon as I embedded her in her group or culture, asked her what her grandmother would have said, I suddenly got an answer. The boyfriend was out of control, with all kinds of psychiatric symptoms. He had lost his bonds with his parents and extended family. There was no one to keep him in check. He had threatened her and her baby with a knife, and walked for hours with them through Amsterdam, the knife hidden under his coat. We had warned her about him, but she just didn't hear it. Through her sister, we managed to contact her mother. Because it was a life-threatening situation, the mother was prepared to cooperate. She called her daughter every day with instructions prompted by us. It helped, the girl started obeying her mother, so she was protected again. Through that experience I became convinced that whenever people are fundamentally 'outbedded' from their family, when that envelope is torn to pieces, they can no longer hear you. In such cases you will have to bring them back to old frames of reference. Once that wrap, that envelope, is put back on, it seems as if the buzz disappears from their ears. These have been very important moments on my path to 'Protective Wraps.'*
>
> *Working with genograms played a major part in giving people protective wraps. By searching together for important pillars of support and figures of authority in the family, people started animated discussions among themselves, and all kinds of memories emerged. All sorts of scenarios unfolded regarding the ways in which we, as care workers, should act in order to align ourselves with the family's decision-making procedures. Suddenly, old patterns surfaced and were redesigned to take a new shape in the Netherlands.*

Wat exactly is 'Protective Wraps'?

'Protective Wraps' means embedment in the culture, in the group. It is very wide-ranging. It is not only about family, but about everything that stems from the past. It's the scents, the landscape, the traditions, the rituals, the history, the food. It's not just about having had such a nice family back then. It's about the familiar ways of the past. There are customs and practices that no longer apply due to migration. Even just talking about it can have a 'protective wraps' effect. Protective Wraps give access to marginalized experiences, hidden memories come to the surface. 'Protective Wraps' vitalizes people who are in a vulnerable phase of transition. Everyone does it really, not only migrants. Looking for pleasant memories, experiences of safety and warmth, during difficult periods. You can do this by looking up your place of birth, your childhood home, or your grandparents' grave. You can play old songs, try to find that friend from high school, eat something your mother used to prepare for you as a treat. Everyone knows it. And when you stop to think about when that need arises, you will realize that it's often at difficult times in your life. In her training sessions, Kitlyn often shows a film about how

Dutch migrants grow old in Australia.³ They are vulnerable, lonely, lose their second language. Some of them have completely lost their way. Distressing images, that often lead to a better understanding of elderly migrants in the Netherlands. You can see those elderly Dutch people come to life again when they celebrate St. Nicolas or dance the polonaise.

Case manager Marthin is a second-generation Moluccan. The story about his father shows how an elderly migrant finds himself in a very vulnerable, layered life phase transition. With age, the pain of loss caused by migration recurs. He has benefited tremendously from 'Protective Wraps'. Marthin also mentions how he deploys the football club to help Moluccans get enveloped.

> *It's nice to work at Bureau Jeugdzorg, but actually I should focus more on elderly Moluccans in retirement homes. Old people who are 100% Moluccan, but are receiving care in a Dutch environment. That was in response to the video about Dutch people in Australia. I also made the link with my father. Because he's on his own now. My mother died seven years ago. Each time I visit my father at his place he's just sitting there. It makes me wonder what goes on in his mind. Last year there was a Moluccan theater group from Indonesia. They came to the Netherlands and performed in a number of places, including Moluccan neighborhoods. They spoke Malay, which my parents used to speak in the old days, so he could understand. That's also a part of enveloping, an element of recognition. I then thought, that should happen more often. My father is a funny man, but absolutely no partygoer. If there's a party somewhere, he'll say that's not for me. At the time of that theater performance, too, he initially said no, I'm not going to go there. But my sister said come on, we'll go by car. We're going to see that performance. And my father, he loved it! You could see that. I thought that was great. Two weeks later, that same group performed in Assen. And guess who went to see them again? My father! On their final evening in the Netherlands, the Assen community had organized a farewell party for them as a surprise. And who do you think was sitting there, right in the middle of the audience? My father! Usually he never wants to go home late. But at midnight he was still there. So that's how it works. It seems like our parents have adapted, but that's only a façade.*
>
> *I have thought about doing something with elderly Moluccans. Homes do have separate wards for elderly Moluccans. But they employ Dutch social workers there, who can never really know how those old people feel about things. For them seeing a son, a daughter or an acquaintance creates a sense of trust. I really feel I have a role to play there.*
>
> *Maybe it's different for my Dutch colleagues. For them it might be an eye-opener. But for me, the idea of 'Protective Wraps' is more like a confirmation. I've been thinking about it a lot, but until now it didn't have a name. I am a board member of a Moluccan football club. We're only a small club. I think we should promote that club, so I had a stall for it at a local market. The club represents a piece of history, which the third and the fourth generation are totally unaware of. And in order to reach the*

---

3   Video 'Growing old far away from home', produced and directed by Marga Kerklaan, 1984.

elderly, I hung up some photographs dating from the early 1960's. All those 70-year-old men turned up. Suddenly, they pictured themselves as teenagers. Then the stories emerged. They were all gathered around my stall. I noticed that the older generation really only talked about the army. Apparently, that goes on and on. The nice thing is that you also bring generations together. Because the grandson suddenly sees hey, that's grandpa! They start to communicate with each other. I do this very deliberately to encourage exchange between generations. This doesn't only hold true for the first, but also for the second generation of Moluccans. Some of them are approaching 65, 70 years of age. They also have a need to be enveloped. It's not so much that they long back for the Moluccas, but rather for the time of the communities where they lived together after migration to the Netherlands. You can reach them by stimulating that feeling. Right now, I am collecting as many photographs as possible of that period. A football club like ours is one of the beacons. Because everyone used to join the football club, and after Sunday school in the Moluccan community at Schattenberg everyone used to go to the football pitch. My son has now made a website about that. In the guestbook, there are people from all over the country. "Greetings from so-and-so. I am from Schattenberg, too, and I used to play football with you." All those memories come to the surface. It serves as a kind of outlet. "

Compose yourself

'Protective Wraps' offers you the opportunity to compose yourself. When radical life phase transitions occur, there is always a period between taking leave of the old and integration of the new; at such times, there is an awareness of loss and there is an awareness of not having something new yet. In this 'liminal' phase, which we will describe in more detail in chapter 5, you are quite naked. So you can then return to the past, in order to recover something familiar, something to warm you. Then you compose yourself and think hey, I feel a bit better. I'm no longer frightened, vulnerable. That enables you to take new steps. At every life phase transition, migrants have to adapt to the fact that things must be dealt with differently than they were in their homeland. When they have a child, when the child becomes an adolescent, when they lose their job, when a partner dies. The former support structures are no longer there. In each life phase transition, the experience of loss caused by the migration recurs. And the awareness of loss of the old patterns and rituals. In that phase, it is important to go looking for things that can be recaptured from the past, in order for you to recover and compose yourself during that vulnerable period.

Kitlyn:

" *In Madagascar, the home country of a colleague of mine, there was a tradition that sons at the age of 14 had to build a small house next to the parental home. Then they had to stay there in order to learn how to become independent. The father and particularly the mother were not allowed to go there. Only the grandmother was*

> *welcome, to utter exhortations, to tell them to clear up their mess, to stop them from drinking or from inviting women. The thought behind this was that the grandparents are in a better position to impose those limits, because there is a little more distance. When my colleague's son reached that age, she said, 'How can I do this here in the Netherlands? I can't just have him building a small house here! How can I help him on his way to adulthood?' At first this was very problematic. She had the idea that doing something similar here was absolutely impossible. It made her apathetic. At some point the two of us started to try and see how we could translate the way things used to be for her there, to the here and now. We came up with the idea of adapting the bicycle shed for daytime use. Nights were too complicated. Her mother then came over for a period of six months. So that's how a way was found to make it easier for her to supervise her son's transition to adulthood.* **"**

The moving story of case manager Jaccoline illustrates how the cold relationship between herself and her in-laws changes as a result of a traumatic event. In that life phase transition, that liminal phase in which everyone is vulnerable, a connection is made possible by Jaccoline letting her in-laws perform their own rituals in her domain. She helps them to embed, thereby allowing the family to compose themselves and to embrace her.

> **"** *Rocky and I have been in a relationship for ten years. Seven years ago, our twins were born, Desi and Daphne. Rocky is Aruban, his father was Surinamese. He comes from a family with six children. The first six years I felt at a distance from his family, although I always went along faithfully. But my mother-in-law's life took place in the kitchen. It was there that her children gathered. And I was always in the living room with the grandchildren. It felt like I wasn't allowed into the kitchen. There seemed to be a certain amount of hostility. The women are absolutely dominant in that family. My contact with my brother-in-law, and also with two of my sisters-in-law, Surinamese and Dutch, was better. They accepted me more easily than the other ladies.*
> *From time to time I thought not to come along. But in the end I always went anyway, for Rocky and the children. Once, I was at a birthday with a barbecue outside. I was sitting at a certain spot with my Dutch sister-in-law. And the circle was built up at some distance away from us. I was literally placed outside the circle. I actually didn't talk to anyone all day, except to Rocky.*
> *When my son was three, he died of meningococci. Overnight. I had had eye surgery, so he was staying with my parents. My mother called to say that he wasn't well. A touch of flu, feverish. When we arrived at my parents' place, we could see that something was terribly wrong. Initially he was taken to the local hospital. From there, he was transferred to Groningen University Hospital, where he arrived at three in the morning. Rocky had the idea that Desi's skin was getting whiter and whiter. That was because the skin was dying, the doctor said. When the doctor told us that he was virtually certain that Desi was not going to make it, we gave permission for him to die. We noticed that every time we left the room, he had a cardiac arrest and had to be resuscitated. But as soon as we entered the room, his heart started to beat again. We had the feeling he was doing it for us. So we sat by his bed and said: you may go. He*

died at six in the morning. Tuesday, 14 May, 2002.

When something like that happens, you get into a very strange state of mind. There's so much to be arranged. All that time we kept in contact by telephone with Rocky's mother. But she only arrived on the Friday, together with her sister, with whom we had been completely out of touch. We had been notified that certain things would have to be done. For them, the family tradition is to keep a vigil during the night before the funeral, to ensure that no spirits enter the grave, so that the deceased is free from spirits for the funeral. It involves certain rituals. For example, for all the children who are the size of the child who died, a blue ribbon must be put in the coffin, to make sure that the deceased does not remain with the living. And there was also a special ritual to free Daphne from Desi, because they were twins. This required for her to be passed over the coffin three times. When all that was announced, I got terribly angry! I said to Rocky, she thinks that after ignoring me for such a long time, not being able to accept me, she can come and do things like that in my house? I don't want that! And then after that I suppose we're to continue on the same footing! He told his mother that. His mother then said that all that was going to change. Things will never be the same again, she said, the contact will change. So I said, all right, if that's the case then it's allowed. But I don't want to have anything to do with it.

They arrived that Friday. They carried out the rituals with Daphne and with Rocky himself there. At one point I also felt my neck being touched. They put alcohol on your neck to protect you from evil spirits. And they kept a vigil all night. At such times a lot of things happen, apparently. But I didn't go into that. It was just too much for me. The next day Desi was cremated.

It has triggered a major transformation in my contact with my mother-in-law. From that moment onwards, she started to really accept me as her daughter-in-law. That has changed enormously since Desi's death. And the sisters-in-law also allow me to join them in the kitchen. The kitchen is a sacred place, where life takes place. So once you're allowed in there, you're accepted. I now feel involved from a distance. For Rocky it was important that those rituals were performed to distance himself. I am very glad that I allowed it. **"**

A biological process

In his article 'Envelopment and the importance of culturally sensitive diagnostics and therapy', psychologist Victor Kouratovsky describes how, from pregnancy, a child is enveloped by language and culture. So even before birth, a child is embedded in 'protective wraps', in order to be able to cope with developments and changes. Because change leads to stress.[4]

Child and adolescent psychiatrist Glenn Helberg tells us that from birth, children learn from their environment how to move from a stressful situation to a restful situation. Strategies for composing oneself are recorded in the brain at the

---

4   Kouratovsky, V. (2008), 'Inwikkeling en het belang van cultuursensitieve diagnostiek en therapie,' In: T.I. Oei en L. Kaiser (eds.), *Forensische psychiatrie onderweg*, pp. 371-385. Nijmegen: Wolf Legal Publishers.

beginning of a human life. There is a biological process aimed at bringing people in a phase of renewed stable equilibrium (homeostasis) at times of stress. Whenever stress occurs, there is a response from the organism. This mechanism is triggered by the pituitary gland, the hypothalamus and the adrenal cortex. Cortisol plays an important part in this. The process looks after the different stages of information processing, namely learning, storage and evocation of behavior patterns.[5]

Thus, your body is equipped to handle stress. The way you are rebalanced as a baby or as a child, is dictated by your environment. After all, as a baby you cannot act on your own. When you start crying, you're held by your mother. When you're hungry, you're fed. When you've had a fall, you get a kiss on the sore spot. These comforts are anchored in your brain, with the associated smells, voices, flavors, colors and impressions of your environment, by means of the biological process described above.

This is how people's resolving power is developed. Sometimes, in the event of multiple loss experiences and trauma, it seems like this power is no longer there. Or that it has been forgotten. In such cases, a care worker can activate the memory of the former problem-solving strategies with the aid of the tools described in chapter 7.

Facilitating 'Protective Wraps'

Frequently, people go looking for protective wraps of their own accord, although they don't realize it. It is important that you as a care worker are aware of how you yourself do that. Because if you're sensitive to it, you can help others along. You can use it as a healing tool. You can facilitate it when making genograms and lifelines, when asking contextual questions, when asking for life stories, old customs, rituals from the past. How solutions used to be found in the past, how decisions were made. And then look for ways to translate all that to the present. Go looking for ways to open the hatch, so you can see faces suddenly light up, a spark starting to glow. What do people need from their old context to enable them to function in the new context? Some Dutch care workers think that it is in fact a good thing to keep the old ways away from migrants, for fear of them remaining stuck in the past. Especially in the case of refugees with traumatic experiences, it is often thought best to let bygones be bygones, so as not to awaken old wounds. But people actually need to carry the burden of the past to enable them to create a place in the future. People don't want to go back. They just want to have a look around in the past in order to develop a perspective for the future.

A film about French transcultural psychiatrist Marie-Rose Moro shows how she shapes 'enveloppement' in her aid to migrants. From various perspectives, a large multicultural group of therapists reflects on clients' stories, dreams and complaints. The group envelops the clients and forms a big warm protective wrap. It helps clients to resume their lives by integrating the problem in the context of their migration history. The client always attends the sessions with his or her direct

---

5   Rijk, R. de, F. Zitman en R. de Kloet (2004), 'Neuro-endocrinologie van de stressrespons'. In: J.E. Hovens, A.J.M. Loonen en L. Timmerman (eds.), *Handboek neurobiologische psychiatrie*. De Tijdstroom.

family, or with other relatives. In the film, a case is presented of an African single mother with two sons. Her youngest cries all the time. By reflecting on her dreams with the group as protective wrap, it was discovered that the mother bears a deep sorrow caused by disruption and loss. The moment Moro indicates that the child is crying because of her sorrow, the child starts screaming. Then at the same time a visible moment of healing takes place. Within that context, the child begins to talk for the first time, it relaxes and starts to play with its elder brother.[6]

Children's complaints are often related to complaints regarding the whole system. Research shows that 80% of children's complaints are related to parents' complaints.[7] Awareness of that, too, is often lacking in the Dutch care perspective. Meeting people together with their families makes it easier to recognize. If people from a collective system are invited for an interview on their own, if they are isolated from their system, they might get confused or even all worked up, because that's not the way it should be in their context. They might not even realize this. They stop switching perspectives and may feel impotent and angry. And yet it is still unusual for people to visit a care worker together with their family. It frequently happens that four children from one family end up with four different therapists. Maddening for all those concerned, but particularly so if you come from a collective system, where the way you function is related to the group. We will deal with this in more detail in chapter 4.

Kitlyn:

> *"A Moroccan man was made to look after the interests of his family. His eldest brother, who used to be the one in charge, had died, and now he was the figure of authority. As the senior, the man suddenly felt very vulnerable. The problem was that his youngest sister's children had all been placed in care, and his sister had returned to Morocco. He worried about her only daughter, who was living with a 'foreign' foster family. Each time the man visited Bureau Jeugdzorg, he went completely out of his mind, screaming and throwing things. I did some research on that girl. But I never want to see people on their own, so I invited the man together with his family in order to tell them about my findings. He arrived with his two sisters. They themselves chose where to sit. One on his one side and the other on his other side. The oldest sister took hold of him every time he started to scream. She said something to him in Berber, whereupon he calmed down. She then said: "He has understood, you may continue." It turned into a very intense conversation, during which the oldest sister kept embedding her brother whenever he flew into a rage. At the end of the interview, the people at Bureau Jeugdzorg were quite amazed by the fact that the three had very accurately expressed their wishes, had explained what was going on in the family, old wounds, and what they were worrying about."*

---

6   Dvd: 'I was dreaming of a large body of water' – Transcultural system therapy: experiences in France of Marie-Rose Moro and her team, filmmaker: Laurence Petit-Jouvet, March 2006.
7   Lecture Keppel Hesselink, 'Quackery or complementary forms of treatment: How to separate wheat from chaff?' Second congress Integrative Psychiatry: *Looking for new opportunities*, Groningen, 9 May, 2007.

This is a perfect example of how people can compose themselves once they are embedded in a safe context. If someone so vulnerable is removed from his family structure and is expected to talk to the care worker on his own, he will stop switching perspectives. He will feel frightened and will no longer listen.

Finally

Now that the core of the term 'Protective Wraps' has been discussed, we will go on to the next chapter, which tells the story of the province of Drenthe. It amazes Kitlyn to note how her story and the story of Drenthe fit together seamlessly. The story about Drenthe shows how elements of southern we-oriented cultures are also latent in the Netherlands. It shows that diversity is also ingrained in the native-born Netherlands culture. Drenthe illustrates that not only migrants, but everyone in the Netherlands, too, carry 'the Other' within them. Hence, the intercultural dialogue applies everywhere.

Assignment

- What are your protective wraps?
- What kind of protective wraps does your family have when life is not easy due to illness, death or problems?
- What kind of protective wraps are there at the training, at your internship or at work?
- In what situation and in what way can you use protective wraps in your profession? Give an example for the Other and for yourself.

3

Diverse Drenthe

"What is typical of Drenthe?" Kitlyn asked one of the managers of Bureau Jeugdzorg Drenthe. She replied: "We say yes to everything. My mother always keeps four brands of coffee in the cupboard, varying in quality. When neighbors come to visit whom she doesn't like very much, she will let them in, but they will get a cup of the cheapest coffee."

Whenever Kitlyn walks into a place, she takes a good look around her. Looking for the stories with their important underlying ideas. What are the cultural characteristics, what are the ideas about diversity, what kind of inclusion and exclusion mechanisms are at work, how about the male-female relationships, the white-black relationships? Because working on diversity is working in uncertainty, working on change. And change always comes with loss. That's why it is important to be very much aware of your own background and identity, so you know with whom you belong, which anchors make you feel secure. As a province, but also as an organization or as an individual. Where are the forces that can be harnessed? And what events, traumas and experiences of loss have occurred that can be rekindled in this phase? This chapter is about the province of Drenthe, about local diversity and ethnicity. Based on the stories of Bureau Jeugdzorg Drenthe employees, the typical characteristics of the province are exposed. Important facts from the past, including the history of the peat colonies and the arrival of the Moluccans, form the current social and cultural landscape. Typical cultural traits such as 'noaberschap' (the unwritten rule to always help your neighbors) and the different dialects, along with the history, accommodate weak spots and powerful features that can be felt beneath the surface. Drenthe shows that integration and adaptation are not only relevant for migrants. Various indigenous cultures must also make the effort to relate to each other on a small part of the Netherlands. Everyone carries a migrant within. The connection between Protective Wraps and phenomena typical for Drenthe turns out to be seamless.

Peat and sand

Drenthe can be roughly divided into two parts: the peat and the sand. There is a traditional rivalry between these two. This is reflected to this day in groups of young people from different villages who are at odds with each other. But the way people classify each other also shows that there are two separate communities that do not necessarily feel related. The river Hunze runs on the border of the Hondsrug (an elongated sand ridge) and the peat. That river is called the 'Daip' by those who live on the peat. They call those who live on the sand 'those folks from the other side of the Daip'. The native communities in Drenthe, the original inhabitants, live on the sand. The villages with the greens surrounded by farms are characteristic of the area. Until well into the last century, livestock farming was the main economic activity. Cattle were originally collected on the greens, where there was a watering hole for cattle, a so-called dobbe. The green also served as a meeting place and a market square for the village. There was a high degree of social cohesion, people were rooted in the village. The sand villages were not poor. People owned mixed businesses with all sorts of stuff. All of them smallholders. During harvest time they worked together. And they also frequently shared a shepherd for the sheep. They were and still are fairly closed communities.[1] Peat inhabitants are originally

---

1   Foorthuis, W.R. en P. Brood (eds.) (2002), *Gids voor cultuur en landschap*. Uitgeverij DE PLOEG.

nomads. They moved from one cultivation site to another. Entire families were peat workers. After cultivation of an area had been completed, they moved on. Workers came from Germany as well as from the Netherlands. In the 19th century, the government created institutions in the peat areas for 'persons lacking in moral conduct and good behavior'. They were put to work on the peatlands. Working conditions were dreadful. Long days were worked under appalling circumstances. Up till the beginning of the 20th century, they lived in turf huts and small houses. Industrialization in the course of the 20th century didn't help. Exploitation of workers led to uprisings. Socialism and communism flourished in the peat colonies. Poverty in the 1930s also led to the relatively large following of the NSB (a Dutch fascist and later Nazi political party).[2]

Language

Drenthe has multiple dialects, multiple languages. And each language always expresses its own views. For example, Dutch is the only language that distinguishes between the concepts of *familie*: extended family, family as a group of blood relatives and relatives through marriage, and *gezin:* nuclear family, family as a group of people generally consisting of father, mother and one or more children. This means that for Dutch people there is a difference between the meaning of those two words, whereas in other languages there is only the one word for family. This tells you something about our views. Language is identity, language is culture. When people have to switch between languages, that implies that they also have to be loyal to the views expressed by those different languages. Commuting between languages is like commuting between cultures.

Tim is a family guardian and he's from Drenthe. He speaks different dialects in various contexts. His story illustrates how language is connected with different loyalties and with different roles you have as a person.

> *"It is typical for people from Drenthe to begin by carefully checking out exactly what they're in for. I encountered a Surinamese woman who knew just what she wanted. As the training progressed, what she said appealed to me more and more. I realized that I myself often come across people who live only 10 km apart, but who in effect speak very different languages. I was born in Meindertsveen. The language of the peatlands is said to be rougher than the language of the sand. When I was 23, I got into a relationship with someone from Hunsingo. Hunsingo is a village on the Hondsrug, and that's sand. I noticed a difference in how people interact with each other there, and the language is also different, while it's only 13 km away. My mother comes from yet another language region, namely Midden-Drenthe, in the center of the province. That's a different language, a different culture. So, in my own family I have three different influences to deal with, even though the area is very small. In my work I also notice that in Zuidoosthoek, the southeastern corner of Drenthe where my work is located, I connect*

---

2   Schaap, P.M. en E. Meijerink (2004), *De nieuwe veenkoloniën*. Ekkers & Paauw.

well with the clients. They make it clear that they look upon me as one of them. On the one hand that's easy. But it is also a major pitfall, as it might cause you to be a bit too close. It quite easily creates a locker room atmosphere. 'And perhaps you'd like a beer.' This sometimes makes it difficult to maintain a professional distance. Because of course I'm also a family guardian. I do make it clear to them that I speak their language. But in order to maintain that distance, I prefer to speak standard Dutch. I have the feeling that when I start using the vernacular at work, I can't make decisions. It's like being in the pub then. I know that in the old days there used to be a lot of drinking going on in the peatlands. There was a great deal of poverty. On Friday afternoons, the boss handed the peat workers their pay packet, and instead of going home dad would go to the pub. Lots of jenever (Dutch gin) was drunk. You still see a great deal of alcoholism around here. That suspicion, that wait-and-see attitude, is something that goes with the peat. It's stronger than caution, it's almost like a rejection. That makes you feel good to be one of them. It works easier that way, you gain confidence faster. I notice that colleagues who are not from Drenthe experience more distance, find it harder to establish contact, need more time to gain trust. So that's nothing to do with the quality of the care worker. I have been living on the sand for 20 years now. People from the sand are somewhat less to the point, less straightforward, less direct. They tend to refer to things in a roundabout way. Peat people are more straightforward in saying what they think of something. The people from the peatlands were always dependent on the peat bosses. That automatically meant that they built up a kind of resistance to authority. Whereas those farmers on the sand had everything well in hand. They were not accountable to anyone. I myself was brought up with the peat language. My mother originally had a different dialect. When she had been visiting her mother, our neighbor could hear that. She suddenly spoke her own dialect again. With us she spoke the peat language. So she frequently had to switch. I have never tried to speak my mother's language or my girlfriend's language. I can understand it perfectly and I think I could speak it, too, but it doesn't seem to fit. It doesn't feel right. It would make me feel a renegade. You're not real then, not yourself. My children speak standard Dutch, but with an accent. That's not a deliberate choice. I notice that less and less dialect is spoken among children. With my wife I speak dialect. Both of us speak our own language. That means that at home I constantly speak two languages. Whenever I call a client from the office, I speak standard Dutch, or at least I try to. Sometimes I get stuck. For example, when my wife is with me at the office, I hardly dare speak dialect. Or whenever she calls me from work. She starts off in Dutch, but after three sentences we find ourselves speaking dialect again. We just cannot do it. We just seem to move in weird circles around each other in such cases. I noticed that many of my experiences correspond with those in the Surinamese community. There are many similarities with the culture I grew up in. There is only a small percentage of migrants in our population and among our clients. Yet, in a different way we are often faced with diversity, which is expressed in the language."

Extended families

Many stories heard during the training sessions show that peat families from Drenthe are actually quite similar to Surinamese families. For example the story of Theo, working at the service department of Bureau Jeugdzorg Drenthe, about the role of grandparents in a family.

> *"There is a difference between families in the northeast of the Netherlands and families in the larger northwestern Dutch cities. The extended families often still function in the traditional sense here. I was frequently involved with providing care in rural Drenthe. It's quite normal there for a grandmother to come along for an interview. Grandfathers and grandmothers play an important role in the upbringing. There was a girl with severe mental disorders. Her parents had invited me as a care worker. To begin with, the girl didn't want any professional care at all. She cut herself, felt very bad about herself. I spoke to her parents at their house while she was in her room playing extremely loud music. Her relationship with her parents was very bad. The parents couldn't get her to go to school, nor could they initially get her to talk to me. At one point, talks between her and me got going, and she even came to my office. I noticed once that her grandfather was waiting outside. So grandpa had been called upon to support her. The grandparents were a bridge between the parents and the child. Once you know that, you can make use of it. The child was eventually taken into care, and her grandfather and grandmother played an important role in bringing that about. The parents could never have achieved that on their own. Now they could assume a more or less passive role while the grandparents, without taking sides, could convince the girl that more help was needed. My role was really only to provide a bit of guidance. To ensure that the spontaneously generated process would lead to the intended purpose. I called upon the grandparents, with all due concern for the parents, who had a strong sense of failure as it was, because they were unable to have that contact. We focused on how all of us together could manage to have the girl accept the help that was very much needed."*

Noaberschap

A typical phenomenon in Drenthe is noaberschap. The habit of helping each other in case of illness, problems, or just whenever it's called for. It's taken for granted that when you live close to each other, you take responsibility for each other. And because in the event of problems people initially tend to look for solutions within their own circle, professional help is generally not sought until quite late. This in turn has to do with that closed attitude, not washing your dirty laundry in public.

Theo:

> *Noaberschap still exists in the villages here. People help each other out. Someone does your shopping when you're ill. Or your neighbor looks after your child if you can't do it yourself. Or mows the grass. It's an age-old tradition. If there is no neighborly help, public services must fill those gaps. I also experienced it in my own street. When I came to live there and wanted to renovate my place, my neighbor immediately offered help. This kind of thing happens without expecting anything in return. Money doesn't come into it. These are things that go without saying. Nothing is previously agreed upon, but you can simply call upon each other. In my work in rural areas, I notice that people turn to assistance quite late, because they benefit from help of this nature for a long time. If someone is ill, it's taken care of by the immediate environment. There's no on-the-spot need for a healthcare provider. Grandfathers and grandmothers also play a major role in the care of children. You come across noaberschap in streets and neighborhoods where people live for long periods of time. Where people are rooted. In my street, you keep seeing the same names. A number of elderly people there are still living independently, which is made possible because their children live close by. And because the neighbors offer a helping hand. You won't easily find that in a starters' neighborhood. It's all to do with a heterogeneous composition of the residents. With people of all generations living in such a neighborhood.*

Coexistence

In 1951, due to political circumstances, 4000 KNIL soldiers and their families came from the Moluccas to the Netherlands. KNIL is the abbreviation for Royal Dutch-East Indies Army, a Dutch army in what is now called Indonesia, which was a Dutch colony until 1949. A large part of these families came to Drenthe. Initially they were housed in residential areas such as Schattenberg, or the former Westerbork camp, a World War II Nazi refugee, detention and transit camp. However, later on, when it turned out that their stay in the Netherlands would be of a less temporary nature than originally planned, housing policy was aimed at integration, and in several locations Moluccan residential communities emerged. In the 1970s, grim events ensued. Radical Moluccan youths twice hijacked a train, they took children and teachers hostage at a primary school, and raided the provincial government building, all of it in Drenthe. These actions caused a number of victims.
These days, appeasement prevails again in the relationship with the Dutch government. The emotions stirred up by these events in Drenthe differ per location. It all depends on the extent to which people were involved. In general, it is felt that the Moluccans are well integrated in Drenthe's society. All the same, the fourth generation Moluccans apparently do not perform well at school, and Moluccans also seem to be poorly represented in the middle and higher levels of the job market.

Case manage Marthin is a second-generation Moluccan.

" It seems like our parents have adapted, but that's really only a façade", he says. On the other hand, he tells with a smile how older Moluccan women in a local Drenthe television program sang along at the top of their voices with a song from singer/songwriter Daniel Lohues in Drenthe dialect. "A week later, the same song was played at a Moluccan association get together, and everyone sang along again. Now isn't that wonderful? Apparently, the Moluccans do have a certain bond with Drenthe. "

He explains that the political history in Drenthe is not only a delicate one, but one that has also divided the Moluccan community. These are sensitive issues that are barely open to discussion. In such cases it is a good thing to play football together, for example. You don't have to talk then. It's purely about the game, and in that way people can still be together. Another typical phenomenon is that many people from Drenthe chose to join the NSB (a fascist political party) in the 1930s. The NSB enjoyed a large following throughout Drenthe, not only among the inhabitants of the peat, but also on the sand. Many families are still dealing with this past, they carry it with them. The consequences are palpable. Families are torn apart, contacts cut off. It's a taboo, it's hardly ever mentioned. Yet it is known which villages were NSB strongholds, who exactly supported the enemy. How can a province continue its peaceful life as a community after such traumatic events? How can enemies coexist: nomads and farmers, the good and the bad from the time of the war, the Moluccans and those from Drenthe? Traditions like noaberschap have an important function in managing to come to terms with history. It's like the way the Surinamese manage to get along with each other, even after the murders of 8 December 1982 and the Surinam Airways disaster in 1989. Unquestioning solidarity, regardless of what has happened. You stand by one another. If somebody is renovating his house, you offer help without being asked. This can also give you a sense of suffocation. People keep dropping in to bring you soup. Another explanation is the sense of 'we're all poor'. In a culture of poverty, where people have had to depend on each other for generations, where there is no perspective, little self-confidence, you sustain each other. That is a form of solidarity where it's us against the world. But it's also a snake pit where you constantly pull each other down, cut each other down to size.

Working on diversity in Drenthe

People from Drenthe know their stories. That gives them a strong identity. Knowing your stories makes you very much aware of who you are. On the other hand, there's a mentality in Drenthe that won't allow you to stand out from the crowd. "We're no big deal." Especially those who come from the peat colonies know the feeling of being excluded very well. From the position of the underdog, being oppressed. Others are in charge. We from Drenthe don't belong to the dominant group. And with that, there are many similarities with minority groups like migrants in the Netherlands.

The first thing Kitlyn noticed after she started working as a trainer at Bureau Jeugdzorg Drenthe, was the low number of native people from Drenthe represented in the management of the organization. Out of the seventeen managers there are three from Drenthe, while the other managers come from elsewhere in the country. While those from Drenthe probably know best what's good for the children from Drenthe, what works best in families from Drenthe. She asked one of the employees from Drenthe why it is that everything at Bureau Jeugdzorg Drenthe is brought in from afar. Staff, but also methodologies such as 'Signs of Safety' and the 'Solution-oriented Approach'. They even bring in a Surinamese trainer from Amsterdam for the diversity project. "Yes, we do tend to have a low opinion of ourselves", was his answer.

In Drenthe there is a feeling of 'we are all equal'. This is how you gloss over differences. As a care worker or as an organization, you create a universal truth that applies to everyone. Everyone can be approached in the same way, because everyone is the same. This approach does not do justice to differences, it does not take diversity into account. Consideration for diversity means paying attention to differences. Being sensitive to diversity implies understanding of gender, religion, ethnicity, age, state of health, and numerous other aspects. But it also means being aware of culture, family, views, history. Working on diversity is working in uncertainty. Nothing is fixed. That is why it is important to know where your strengths lie. Because how do you keep yourself going? It is also important to know what your sacred cows are, which views you have yourself that do not correspond with your client's views. And whether you can manage to put these on hold for a while. Just say goodbye to your own convictions for a moment. So that you can keep the dialogue going. You used to learn that as a care worker you always know best. But there you are now, ignorant before a family. This means that you must ask a lot of questions. It is essential for care providers working with 'Protective Wraps' that they are aware of the pitfalls and the strengths. For care workers in Drenthe, it is therefore important to know whether someone is from the peat or from the sand, to give an example that is typical for Drenthe. Because not everyone is the same, and the existence of a blueprint for helping to solve a certain problem is an illusion.

Superdiversity, inclusion and exclusion

With the help of the following three concepts, you can teach yourself to look at reality in a different way from what you're probably used to.

Superdiversity

Superdiversity is a term that is gaining ground in Belgium and in the Netherlands. It has been described by Dirk Geldof[3], Maurice Crul and others[4]. It is being introduced as a new term to describe our societies, because the terms diversity and multiculturalism no longer suffice.

---

3   Geldof, D. (2015), *Superdiversiteit, hoe migratie onze samenleving verandert*. Leuven: Acco.
4   Crul, M. et al. (2013), *Superdiversiteit*, Elitesproject.eu.

In half a century, we have grown from a society with a limited extent of ethnic-cultural diversity to an immigration society. Native-born people from Amsterdam, for example, are a minority group in the city. And of Amsterdam youngsters up to the age of fifteen, only a third can still be called native Dutch. In the cities in particular, successive waves of migration have resulted in a highly complex social reality. Diversity within diversity is considerable.

Due to transmigration[5], with multiple countries of origin and arrival, and with bi-cultural partnerships and composite families being commonplace, there is no longer a clear answer to the questions: what is your culture and where are you from? Us-them thinking has become quite meaningless, because them has become us and we are all linked to a migration history and multiple cultures. It is better for us to move towards and-and thinking. This reality requires a great deal of curiosity and involvement from care workers, because one just never knows, so one will have to keep asking.

Doxa[6]

Doxa is a concept that helps to unravel inclusion and exclusion in human systems, for example in the workplace or in a family. You can picture it as a box made up of beliefs, put together by a group of people who are very similar to each other. Everything that does not fit into the doxa remains outside. It is a totally unconscious process. In order to break open a doxa, the layers it consists of will have to be analyzed. What is the dominant group? What are the beliefs of this group? What doesn't fit in? By shining the light on 'the Others' in the dominant group, space is created for 'the Others' from outside the group. Exchanging stories and histories is essential in this respect.

An example is that teams in youth care organizations often consist of young white women. It is comfortable, because everyone thinks and acts pretty much the same way. The question is whether this meets the client's needs, and whether you create space for 'the Others' in your organization. How simple is it to operate in such a team for a black man with different views on good care?

To create space for 'the Others' in the doxa, it helps to explore and to share the peculiar and nonstandard properties of each person in the dominant group. In doing so the dominance of the doxa is challenged.

A good example is the Dutch television program *Over de streep* (Across the line). This program demonstrates in secondary schools that everyone has a story. After a safe atmosphere has been created, everyone in the group is invited in an accessible way to show or tell something personal. Untold stories are revealed. Children talk about their addicted father, their abused mother, their grandmother who died, their criminal brother, their grief and loneliness. Stories which are really too painful for children to tell, but which have made them precisely into who they are. In class, things that were never known before are shared for the first time. On

---

5   Geldof, D. et al. (2015), *Transmigratie, hulp verlenen in een wereld van superdiversiteit*. Leuven: Acco.
6   Bourdieu, P. (2001), *Masculine domination*. Cambridge: Polity Press.

closer inspection, not five but fifty children cross the line when asked whether they feel lonely. And by sharing this with each other, everyone becomes vulnerable: the dominant group, the bullies, the odd ones out. This creates attention, understanding and compassion for each other. Teachers, too, show a different side of themselves and participate in the process. All of them carry 'the Other' inside them. This invariably leads to a tremendous feeling of solidarity.

To break open a doxa with the aim of creating space for diversity, it's important to analyze the layers the doxa consists of. And, as pointed out above, it also helps to create awareness of the presence of 'peculiar and nonstandard' properties, besides the dominance. In a context where highly educated left-wing white men play a decisive role, you can go looking for the characteristics these men display that do not fit into the doxa. For example a disability, a great loss, fatherhood. By shining the light on 'the Other' among the members of the dominant group, space is created for the admission of 'the Others' from outside the group.

Crossroad thinking

The concept of intersectionality, developed by Afro-American scientists, provides a dynamic model for unraveling dimensions of diversity. The model was introduced in the Netherlands as *Crossroad Thinking*[7] by Gloria Wekker, professor of gender and ethnicity. The crossroad signifies a convergence of a number of axes, each representing a different personal or social definition. Think of gender (from male to female), ethnicity (from black to white), class (from rich to poor), age (from young to old), degree of health (from disabled to healthy) and sexual preference (from homosexual to heterosexual). The difference with diversity thinking is that the latter often uses fixed terms. You are white, you are homosexual, or you are disabled. While the axes of crossroad thinking require a score on a sliding scale. So you can be female, rich, religious to a greater or lesser extent. But you can also come from a collective family system or have a migration history to a greater or lesser extent. The history and organization of the family system and the migration history are important aspects of 'Protective Wraps' in identifying differences between people. Crossroad thinking provides room for nuances, thus reducing the risk of stigmatization and stereotyping.

Communitas

The training sessions conducted by Kitlyn for the employees at Bureau Jeugdzorg Drenthe were the place where the stories in this book were first told. It was there that the similarities between the characteristics of Drenthe and the principles of 'Protective Wraps' became apparent. That was the place of the eye-openers about the personal history of many of the care workers, but also about the practical provision of care. The training sessions were important as a basis for embedding diversity

---

7   Wekker, G. (1998), 'Gender, identiteitsvorming en multiculturalisme: notities over de Nederlandse multiculturele samenleving', In: K. Geuijen (ed.), *Multiculturalisme*. Lemma.

thinking at Bureau Jeugdzorg Drenthe. In order to hold on to the stories, ideas and experiences that came to the surface there, the idea for this book was born. The way in which Kitlyn gives shape to her training sessions offers important leads for intercultural care efforts. That is why something is explained about it here.

In the communication between care worker and client, security and trust are preconditions. During the training sessions, too, a sense of security is needed in order to learn to look at things from a different perspective. Kitlyn found that she could connect well with the students once she herself adopted a humble attitude. Being the authority, but at the same time also showing the vulnerability of her own family in the contact with others. If you feel safe, you are less afraid to share experiences that you are ashamed about or have hidden away. For that reason, it is important that there is no emotional confusion.

A theoretical concept that describes the atmosphere that is often created during Kitlyn's training sessions is *communitas*.[8] Communitas is a concept from cultural anthropology and the social sciences. It represents an intensive community spirit, the sense of a high degree of social equality, solidarity and togetherness. It transcends an ordinary social situation in more ways than one. Because in a safe situation people share intimate and important experiences with each other, a feeling is created of invulnerability, sanctity, a sacred place. There is optimal concentration for listening to each other's stories. That is what often happens when people start telling each other life stories. A kind of holy place arises, where healing can take place. It regularly happens that people right there and then start to mourn experiences of loss, which will lead to healing. You should be able to facilitate that particular atmosphere for your client as well.

A number of employees about the training sessions:

Case manager Jaccoline:

> *"I especially remember how important your own socialization is in relation to your work. I liked that being pointed out to me. What is your own upbringing, your own life, doing with you in your work at this moment? The influence of your childhood, your parents and beyond, your grandparents. How has that shaped you and how does it affect your clients? What are you bringing along and what is your client bringing along from his or her background? As a result, I talk much more to clients about how they were raised, the influence of that on their current lives and on how they raise their children."*

Location manager Jan:

> *"What stuck with me most about the training is the dominant convictions of families. We automatically think: there is Dutch culture and there are other cultures. But that is a misconception. After I had done the training, I knew what interculturality is all*

---

[8] Turner, V.W. (1969), The ritual process: Structure and anti-structure.

> *about, namely that two people meet up. All human beings have their own culture. And each culture has its own dominant conviction.*

Service department employee Theo:

> **"** I have experienced the training in a very positive way. It meant staying very close to yourself. The training started by looking at your own origins, where you're from. Or, as they say in Drenthe, roughly translated: "From where are you one of?" The training made me realize what you bring in yourself. And that your own origin has a lot of influence on how you approach your migrant clients. You think there are many differences, but you turn out to have a lot in common. For me that was an eye-opener. And that in the Netherlands, too, in addition to your own nuclear family, others can play a role when you have problems. You are part of a larger context. **"**

Finally

Drenthe illustrates that in the Netherlands, too, there are diverse cultures, local historical influences, different views, languages and loyalties. We all carry a migrant within us. Parallels can be drawn between coexisting with one another and coexisting with migrants. Being aware of diversity in your own circle leads you to a greater understanding of 'the Other'. After all, the intercultural dialogue also takes place close to home. Part of local diversity is reflected in the uniqueness of each family. It is important to gain insight into the way your own family and your client's family are built up. What is the history, the structure, who are the figures of authority, what are the dominant views? The next chapter is about families. We-oriented family systems and I-oriented family systems. Knowledge and understanding of this are essential for the intercultural dialogue.

Assignment

- On the basis of this chapter, can you give an example of a situation in your study program, at your internship or at work, where there is inclusion and where there is exclusion? Which mechanisms are at work here?

4

The strength of families

Kitlyn: "Making an issue of the importance of families should be seen here within the context of the Netherlands. If you ask an Iranian about his family, he might be able to sum up everyone who lived up to as many as five generations ago. In certain milieus in Iran, the names of all the ancestors are etched on a large bar which hangs next to the front door."

Throughout history, the Netherlands has had to deal with a loss of family awareness. This is due to all kinds of historical developments, such as the secularization and the individualization of society. It has become the norm to base your choices in life on your own insights and to not let them depend on church, family, employer or neighborhood.[1] You don't choose your family. Your family is a given, whether you like it or not. Your family has an impact on your life. In a positive sense, in a negative sense, or both. Families are very important. Families provide a protective system. Families carry wisdom within them, which is important for your identity. Family stories give you access to the healing of wounds. And families provide a safe place for children to grow up. Families are often overlooked when seeking solutions for children who end up in youth care. While the key to children's happiness is often to be found in their own circle.

As a care worker, you can use the strengths of families to tackle a particular problem. Because families themselves know best what is good for their children. In the Netherlands, this is a considerable blind spot; it's a struggle for us to accept it. This chapter therefore focuses on families. So that you, as a care worker, will gain more insight into the self-healing capacity of families, and will be able to act as a facilitator. What is the difference between we-oriented families, as in most southern cultures, and more I-oriented families like in the Netherlands? How does communication take place within the families? What are the views on families in the Netherlands, and how did these views come about? What does raising children involve in the Netherlands, and what critical comments can be made? Why is it so important to focus on multi-generation families, what is the added value? What does the concept of family continuity mean, and what are the important beliefs within families? And why is it beneficial to call on families to take care of children who cannot live with their own parents? Stories and anecdotes illustrate how families are structured and how they function, both in I-oriented systems and in we-oriented systems.

Two families thrown together

Location manager Jan talks about his wife and children, his relatives and his wife's relatives. His story shows how families from the Netherlands and from Indonesia have different characteristics and views.

> *"My wife is from Indonesia. That's evident at every turn. Where our views are concerned, we're sometimes totally at odds with each other. She believes that you should always be prepared to help others. That's really a typical Asian trait. I have been to Indonesia myself. You see it everywhere there. Everyone is always there for you. Even though they have nothing, in the end there's all kinds of food on the table. They want to please you in every possible way. We sometimes have people visiting us, and a tremendous amount of shopping has to be done. Then I occasionally can't*

---

[1] Dijkstra, P.A., *Het zit in de familie*. Oration on the occasion of the acceptance of the chair of Relationship Demographics at the University of Utrecht, 29 October 2003.

help thinking 'for crying out loud'. We get along just fine all the same. We have been happily married for a very long time. It's the same with her family; I see the same thing at her sister's and her mother's. Always being there for someone else, always wanting to please others. Mind you, it's also very nice and very good. I was brought up with the notion that the most important thing is to take good care of yourself. To make sure that you never have to depend on someone else. When you visit my family, it's clear that all of them have taken good care of themselves. I'm from a large family and most of them have their own businesses. I myself have a managerial function, which also implies a certain independence. We may have gone a little too far in taking good care of ourselves. I have a daughter and a son. I see myself conveying my ideas to them. Take good care of yourself and see to it that you don't need anyone else. But they also get my wife's share. So, you should not only take good care of yourself, but you should also be prepared to help others. Because some day you might need someone else yourself. I notice that my daughter mainly picks up my message. She will no doubt take good care of herself. She is living with someone who is away four days a week. Would you make such a choice inadvertently? I think that my son is more likely to take care of us, his parents. Quite extraordinary. After my wife's knee surgery, it was my son who offered to cook for us twice a week. My daughter wouldn't have done that. She would have suggested having something delivered.

Things sometimes surprise me. For example, my wife says we're going to see a friend in The Hague. For me that's a trip around the world. But OK, friends are family. I had to get used to that. I also had to figure out exactly how things work. Who is Aunt Lien? Well, she turned out to be someone who once met my mother-in-law in Indonesia. And now she has come to the Netherlands. Then I think how nice it is that you can consider someone like that as family. It would never occur to me. When we were in Indonesia, it also happened that we came across family I didn't know. There was me trying to figure it out again. How can that be? Surely, they cannot be family. Later I thought, never mind. It's of no importance whether or not it's a blood relative. It's simply family, period! My mother-in-law is 80 years old, so her lady friends and all those aunts are about the same age. I think the way they get along is wonderful. You perceive a kind of closeness. The fact that people just have that quality, I think that's great to see. Sometimes they lose sight of each other for ten or twenty years, but that doesn't matter at all. There are always things to be discussed, they share a lot. I grew up with the idea that you shouldn't share everything. At birthday parties, I'm sometimes really racking my brain for something to talk about. But whenever I'm with my in-laws, that doesn't matter. There are always people asking me how I'm doing. Even though they don't know me well, I am included in the family, I'm part of it. And I liked that experience. Still, at times you have to get used to it. Because the other side of the story is that it creates obligations. I don't have a lot of obligations towards my family. But if one of my wife's aunts is ill, you simply must go there. You can't say that it's not convenient right now. But they do appreciate it, and there's always something to eat waiting for you. **"**

I-oriented systems and we-oriented systems

As Jan's story shows, there is a big difference between cultures as regards views and family structure. There are, of course, many nuances to be considered in the way in which families throughout the world are organized. Moreover, the world is constantly changing and it's not quite as black and white as we have outlined here. Migration and globalization lead to an increasing mixture of cultures and patterns. But roughly two types of systems can be distinguished. And because it helps one to understand the Other, we will describe the two most extreme forms. The I-oriented system, with the focus on the individual, and the we-oriented system, with the focus on the interests of the group. Over the last twenty years, the concepts 'I-cultures' and 'we-cultures' have increasingly been taught and used in the intercultural care sector. The terms touch upon the scientifically elaborate concept of the 'Ich Wir Balance' by Norbert Elias.[2] Geographically, it can be said that the characteristics of the I-oriented system prevail mainly in families in Western societies. Families in other countries are organized predominantly according to the we-oriented system.[3]

Many migrants in the Netherlands come from we-oriented families, and it is particularly those groups we have in mind when we talk about a we-oriented system. But in the previous chapter it became clear that in Drenthe, too, elements of the we-oriented system still prevail in families, especially on the peatlands. As we already noted, there is no clear line to be drawn.

The Western nuclear family, consisting of parents and children as a unit, with the well-being of the children as its main theme, is a relatively recent organizational model for families. Nevertheless, this form is the norm in the Netherlands, and the provision of care is also focused on this model.[4] The divide between the collective and the individual system offers important tools for a care worker to understand the behavior of 'the Other', and thus to be able to make use of the strengths of the system. That is why we are listing the most important features here.

The collective we-oriented system

Important themes in the collective system are the observance of authority, relational dependence, and giving shape to family continuity.[5] Rituals and authority structures ensure that it is completely clear how extended families interact within three or four generations. The survival of the family is paramount, everyone is equipped for that. So, if there is a calamity in the family, if someone dies or people lose their job, you will see that every household will change composition in no time at all. Because everyone will start taking care of each other's children right away. They support each

---

2   Norbert, E. (1987), *Die Gesellschaft der Individuen*. Frankfurt a. M.
3   Jessurun, C.M. (2004), 'Hoe meer verschillen, hoe meer vreugd'. In: R. Beunderman, A. Savenije, M. Mattheijer en P. Willems (eds.), *Meer kleur in de jeugd-GGZ*. Assen: Koninklijke Van Gorcum.
4   Ende, M. van den en A. Savenije (2002), 'Zwijgen versus spreken, Geheimen als copingsmechanismen bij bi-culturele adolescenten', *Tijdschrift voor systeemtherapie*, nr. 14, pp. 229-243.
5   Lau, A, (1995), 'Gender; power and relationships, Ethno-cultural and religious issues'. In: C. Burk and B. Speed (eds.), *Gender, power and relationships*. London: Routledge.

other financially and emotionally. After migration, there are an awful lot of changes. But what doesn't change is the support structure.[6] Despite complex circumstances, people will continue to take care of each other and each other's children. Within the family there are always figures of authority. These differ per culture and per family.[7] In a matriarchy women, for example the eldest daughter, will play an important role in decision-making. In Kitlyn's story we saw that her mother, her eldest sister and herself made the important decisions for the family. In a patriarchy, where men are in charge, the decision-makers can be the eldest son, or the husband of the eldest daughter. Decision-making structures are passed down from generation to generation. Positions of authority can change over the years, depending on events such as divorce, criminal activity or migration, which require the creation of a new order. Positions of authority can also be acquired through certain qualities and social positions held by a person. This is also how Kitlyn acquired her position of authority in the family. Growing up as a child in a we-culture is fundamentally different from growing up in an I-culture. In a we-culture you derive your strength as a child from the contribution you make to the system, not from your personal performance. Children are often raised by multiple caregivers, such as mothers, aunts, uncles, grandparents and older siblings. Children sleep together and take care of each other. They have an economic function, and eventually will take care of their parents and other relatives, also financially. From a young age, the child is involved in adult activities. The baby is usually taken along everywhere, while the mother simply continues her own activities.[8]

The individual I-oriented system

In an I-oriented system, individual independence, autonomy, right of self-determination, self-fulfillment and privacy are paramount. Autonomy is more important to mental well-being than social responsibility and interconnectedness. Children are brought up on the basis of that autonomy-thinking, with the assumption that it is possible to be separated from others. Parents and child are supposed to let go of each other in the adolescent phase, after a very loving and extremely careful upbringing. The parent-child relationship is central. Parents are the only ones who are allowed to make decisions concerning the child. From a very young age, children are stimulated to form their own opinions and make their own decisions. Children are not by definition required to adapt to their environment, but the environment is adapted to the children. Children are protected from knives, sockets and other dangers that may lie in wait. They are not taken along to grown-up activities, but adults try to participate in children's activities as much as possible.[9]

---

6   Venema, T. (1992), *Famiri Nanga Kulturu, Creoolse sociale verhoudingen en Winti in Amsterdam*. Amsterdam: Het Spinhuis.
7   Tjin A Djie, K. (2000), 'Ouderschap in een wij-systeem', Second Alice van der Pas Lecture.
8   Jessurun, C.M. (2004), 'Hoe meer verschillen, hoe meer vreugd'. In: R. Beunderman, A. Savenije, M. Mattheijer en P. Willems (eds.), *Meer kleur in de jeugd-GGZ*. Assen: Koninklijke Van Gorcum.
9   Jessurun, C.M. (2004), 'Hoe meer verschillen, hoe meer vreugd'. In: R. Beunderman, A. Savenije, M. Mattheijer en P. Willems (eds.), *Meer kleur in de jeugd-GGZ*. Assen: Koninklijke Van Gorcum.

Communication styles

Within I-oriented systems, ideal communication is open, explicit and direct. Many migrants from we-oriented cultures have great difficulty with the way in which the Dutch communicate. Van den Ende[10] indicates, for example, that Muslim communities think our style is rude. "They use more of an indirect, covert style of communicating, that is implicit, intuitive and sensitive towards others. When addressing emotionally sensitive matters, they prefer to speak in proverbs, metaphors and using folk parables. Conflicts are not expressed: they communicate on the basis of what others expect from them." You will find this type of communication in most we-cultures. Dutch care workers frequently feel that their migrant clients distort reality and carry secrets. From a Western perspective, such behavior is not tolerated. This is one of the sacred cows of an I-system, while from the we-perspective it offers a respectful way of dealing with conflicts and of limiting dishonor and shame in difficult and complicated matters.[11] There are also differences in preference for verbal and nonverbal communication. People from Asian countries in particular feel uncomfortable if a verbal response is constantly asked from them, meaning they have to reveal themselves. In their cultures, body language is far more important.[12] In Dutch families you may also encounter this preference. For example, with people from peatlands or clay grounds.

Families in the Netherlands

The Netherlands doesn't like families. In the 1950s and 1960s, many people rejected their families. Because of the oppressiveness. To get away from religion. However, the desire for autonomy has reached proportions that are not consistent with reality. Because you're not on your own as a human being. People are social beings. People want to exchange. People want to be recognized and acknowledged. And people want to belong. So, it is unrealistic to think that you can go through life alone, and that that is the highest goal you can pursue. People think they are living a reality that is not the reality of life.

Kitlyn:

> *"When I ask a student: "With whom in your family do you make decisions?", I get the answer: "I decide on my own." Together with the student I then draw a picture of his family and ask: "Suppose your mother has to go into a nursing home, who is involved in such a case?" Answer: "Oh yes, now that you mention it. My brother will call, and one of my sisters, and such and such, and my sister always does that and my brother*

---

10   Ende, M. van den en A. Savenije (2002), 'Zwijgen versus spreken, Geheimen als copingsmechanismen bij bi-culturele adolescenten', *Tijdschrift voor systeemtherapie*, nr. 14, pp. 229-243.
11   Ende, M. van den en A. Savenije (2002), 'Zwijgen versus spreken, Geheimen als copingsmechanismen bij bi-culturele adolescenten', *Tijdschrift voor systeemtherapie*, nr. 14, pp. 229-243.
12   Arends, A.M. (1998), 'Het ondergesneeuwde lichaam', *Tijdschrift voor Sociale Psychiatrie*, 51, pp. 13-25.

always takes care of that..." In this way, seven or more people can come into the picture who help in making decisions. Or I ask: "Gee, I see you have such and such a quality. Who within your family has that same trait?"[13] At first they say that they are the only one in the family with that particular trait. But once I start looking for it in the family picture, it turns out that there are another ten or so. **"**

The way people see themselves as part of a family in the Netherlands is inconsistent with reality. And that also means you lose something. It must all come from you yourself. Everything comes straight at you. Protection must be found within yourself. There is no group offering you protection. That is why people in the Netherlands are more anxious. If you belong somewhere, or if you can call upon someone, there will be less anxiety. Autonomy implies that you must be in control, that you are the only one responsible, which puts a heavy burden on individuals. Families are important, since they provide a protective system. You derive your identity from them. A recent study has shown that you don't just carry your own experiences with you in this life. Traumas from previous generations, such as hunger, war and poverty, are also stored in your DNA. Experiences of your grandparents and great-grandparents can influence your current life.[14]

Parenting in the Netherlands

Children in collective systems have a functional value for the family, while children in individual systems have a psychological value for parents.[15] Parenting in the Netherlands is tough. Children are completely dependent on that one father and that one mother. The parents are also the only ones for the child to obey. There is no other country in Europe where so many mothers choose to stay at home with their children instead of entering the job market.[16] This is based on the view that the well-being of the child is related to the quality of the mother. And not to the efforts of an extended family. That is typically Dutch. Mothers suffer from this. Mothers feel guilty all the time.

Kitlyn:

" *When I started off as a social worker in the late 1970s, I heard mothers complain about feelings of guilt all the time. After two sessions, I thought there must be no more of this. Over and over I heard my colleagues say how badly those mothers were looking after their children. While all the time I was thinking, but where are the grandparents?*

---

13 Hooft, L., 'Collega's met familietrekjes. Hoe gezinspatronen zich herhalen op je werk', *VB Magazine*, December 1998.
14 This study was reported on in a *Netwerk* program on 23 April 2006.
15 Kagitçibasi, C. (1996), *Family and Human development across cultures. A view from the other side*. Mahwah, NJ: Lawrence Erlbaum.
16 Cuyvers, P. (2006), 'The Netherlands: tolerance and traditionalism'. In: James Georgas, John W. Berry, Fons J.R. van de Vijver, Cigdem Kagitçibasi and Ype H. Poortinga (eds.), *Families across cultures. A 30 Nation Psychological study*, pp. 410-419. Cambridge: Cambridge University Press.

> *I couldn't make sense of these phenomena from the perspective of my Surinamese background.* "

Kitlyn explains how, as someone who comes from a we-culture, she experiences with amazement the fact that the responsibility for children in the Netherlands lies nowhere else than with the father and the mother:

> "*When you are at a sandpit with a number of other adults, then that one particular father or mother must come all the way from the other side to address his or her own child. My son Robin could at times make three other children cry in one fell swoop. While I was on the other side of the playground near the swings. I saw it and thought, those people around there will solve it. Well, no way. I had to come all the way from the other side of the playground to have a word with my son.* "

Single mothers

In youth care, for the most part it's single mothers you come across. Research shows that the black sheep in Dutch families are mainly the single mothers. They are the ones least supported by families, less than single fathers.[17]

Kitlyn:

> "*I ran into that as early as 1977. And we kept muddling along with those mothers. They had to acquire social skills, pedagogical skills, and skills in many more areas. Whereas what they really needed was a solid family network, which is confirmed by this research.* "

In September 2005, an article by Xandra Schutte was published in *de Volkskrant* about motherhood gone berserk in the Netherlands: 'Mother is the key to your success.'[18] A quote: "(...) the present social insecurity with regard to parenting affects the self-confidence of mothers. The makeable child is primarily seen as a vulnerable one, who is extremely sensitive to the consequences of parental incompetence. The result is that these days, mothers even get desperate about something really ordinary like crying." According to the article, parenting is no longer just about health and happiness. The future of our children must be a success, and maternal commitment is the key to that success. Because children in the Netherlands grow up in small families, they don't learn how to deal with different positions. You only have that one father, that one mother, and maybe that sister. They only get that one single angle imprinted. While there is added value in learning to conduct and position yourself in a variety of situations. For single mothers, this means that if you create a loving environment with a number of adults, this will not only protect and

---

17 Komter, A. en T. Knijn (2004), 'Zwarte schapen in de familie', *DEMOS*, vol. 20, nr. 10.
18 Schutte, X., 'Moeder bepaalt je succes', *de Volkskrant*, 17 September 2005.

help the mother, but it will also serve to prevent patterns from repeating themselves. Imprinting the child does not only come from the mother. That is why crèches are a good thing. Because you allow children to have more educators than just their own parents. And you allow parents some relief from that arduous task.

Attention to fathers

It's often the children of single mothers who need help and support. That implies that the father in question plays little or no role in the care and upbringing. After all, following a divorce, children usually end up living with the mother and there is a contact arrangement with the father. One may also wonder what relationship there is between the child's problems and the absence of a father. In any case, it is important to involve the father in the provision of care, even if it's not in the mother's interest. Until not so long ago, this view was tantamount to sacrilege.

Kitlyn:

> *"There were intake forms that didn't even mention the father at all. And if the mothers did not want to involve the fathers, care workers would go along with that for reasons of privacy. But I thought that we, as care workers, should think from the child's point of view. In order to protect the privacy of the mother, half the child's lineage was simply cut away. While that half might just contain the help and support the child needed."*

Various figures indicate that there is a relationship between the absence of a father and the development of problem behavior in children. Investigation into the riots in London in the summer of 2011 showed that the majority of the young people who were arrested grew up without a father. The number was three times higher than the national average in the United Kingdom.[19] And the Amsterdam youth care organization Spirit conducted a target group analysis based on a sample of 145 children who in 2011 called on more serious forms of care. 72% of these children came from a family situation where the biological father was absent.

Various studies have shown that fathers contribute to the development of children in their own specific way.[20] Boys in particular benefit from male role models. Mothers mainly teach children to relax, to care, to find comfort in cuddles, to eat and to talk. Fathers teach children to act, to have confidence, to feel safe in tricky situations by engaging in exciting, sometimes risky and pioneering activities. Think of the father who throws his child into the air: that's the way to teach children that they are safe despite the scary situation. You need both masculine and feminine strategies to be able to stand on your own two feet in life.

It is always important to contemplate the father's role in relation to culture and

---

19 In: The trumpet.com, 19 April 2012.
20 Tavecchio, L. en H. Bos (eds.) (2011), 'Pedagogiek, wetenschappelijk forum voor opvoeding, onderwijs en vorming', *Thema: Vaderschap, rol van vaders in opvoeding van kinderen en diversiteit in vaderschap* 31 nr. 1. Van Gorcum.

migration history.[21] For example, a Moroccan father in the original context may well be the head of the family, but his mother is the head of the extended family, because the role of a Moroccan mother changes as soon as she has grandchildren. From that time, she occupies the highest position in the hierarchy and leads the family. After migration with his family, far away from his mother, a Moroccan father lacks this family support.[22]

To this day, fathers in Afro-Caribbean communities are rarely involved in the upbringing of their children, not even in their country of origin. In the days of enslavement, after the forced migration from Africa, they were completely isolated from their children; there was no normal family life. This pattern has become anchored in the culture.[23]

Fortunately, increasing attention is paid to the importance of fathers for the development of children, and care workers, too, are increasingly aware of this.

Intergenerational family thinking

In the Netherlands, when thinking about families the emphasis is on two generations. The liberating 1960s caused a shift of attention on the part of the highly educated, so also among researchers. Families were in your way. In order to be liberated, you first of all had to liberate yourself from your family dogmas. As a result, multigenerational research came to a standstill, and no further knowledge was developed in that field. Until recently, scientists always focused on partner relationships and on parent-child relationships. In the care practice, too, attention was centered on this field. The scant regard for this aspect in scientific research reflects the trend in society towards a lack of interest in multigenerational families. In 2004, for the first time since the 1960s, research focused on family relationships within and between several generations. It was decided to research the structure of families over several generations for the following reasons.[24] In the first place, it provides insight into how family roles are fulfilled. For example, how did your own parents influence your parenting? Secondly, does the generation you belong to determine your approach to life? Parents who are still alive influence the choices you make. Finally, the family offers a unique place in which several generations are represented within one context. In the Netherlands, people tend to spend their time with their peers. This offers an optimal climate for the development and perseverance of stereotypical ideas and beliefs.[25] Families give children the opportunity to learn to position themselves in various places with different generations. To hold their own in all kinds of situations they encounter in life. And

---

21 Tjin A Djie, K. en I. Zwaan (2015), ' Vaderschap in relatie tot familie cultuur en historie', *Tijdschrift Kinder- en Jeugdpsychotherapie*, vol. 42, nr. 4.
22 Zwaan, I. (2013), *De afwezige vader bestaat niet, en waarom vaders niet moeten moederen*. Amsterdam: Prometheus Bert Bakker.
23 Girigori, O.J. (2015). *Father Absence: The consequences for reproductive behavior and mating strategies among females*. University of Groningen.
24 Dijkstra, P. en A. Komter (2004), 'Hoe zien Nederlandse families eruit?' *DEMOS*, vol. 20, nr. 10.
25 Dijkstra, P. en A. Komter (2004), 'Hoe zien Nederlandse families eruit?' *DEMOS*, vol. 20, nr. 10.

perhaps to be tolerant of multiple views. After all, successive generations tend to represent different views. Research indicates that families in the Netherlands still fulfill important functions. In the first place, the opportunities people get in life are determined mainly by their childhood home situation. And from generation to generation they tend to do well, or otherwise. Family atmosphere, a person's involvement in the wider circle of family relationships, as well as being married, apparently have a significant influence on the chance of someone developing criminal behavior.[26] Secondly, it is still common for family members to be committed to each other, to stand up for each other. They still provide a protective system. Finally, the family is still a major binding agent in society. It has emerged that people who have a relationship and/or children are less likely to commit suicide than single people.[27]

Family continuity

Families are ancient, they are as old as humanity. That is why there is a lot of strength in families. Families have been through everything before. All those experiences are stored in the collective memory. Families have a mission. First and foremost, that mission is aimed at the survival of the family. We call that family continuity. In we-oriented systems this is explicit, but in I-systems it has been snowed under by autonomous thinking. But even if it is not visible, it is there all the same. It is universal for families to have shared common beliefs, whether it's about religion, about rituals, or about raising children. Ideas on how you think children should grow up, with whom, and with what kind of norms and values. The idea of 'we always do it this way', the dominant view in a family. Those are sacred cows. And that is why it is often considered very important that partners are found in like-minded families. To ensure the survival of the family. A partnership is successful when the other person is someone from the same group with the same rituals. Arranged marriages and keeping a woman's hymen intact until marriage are also aimed at preventing discontinuation of the family. Each family has its black sheep. Those are the ones who are disloyal to the dominant view of the family. They don't act 'the way we always do'. Depending upon the strategies you, as the black sheep, have to keep the conversation with the dominant group going, you will stay connected to your family to a lesser or greater degree. Sometimes it is necessary to force a temporary break. But to disconnect completely from your family means that you give up on the connection with your roots. No matter what, you will always remain an offshoot of that family tree. In your genes and in history, you are connected with your ancestry. To be wrenched away from your basis will lead to loss of identity. Because however much you deviate, by birth you are energetically connected to that group. The prints are in your genes. An example of

---

26 Dijkstra, P. en H. de Valk (2007), 'Criminelen in de familie, Verband tussen crimineel gedrag en bevolkingskenmerken onderzocht', *DEMOS*, vol. 23, nr. 1.
27 Dijkstra, P.A., *Het zit in de familie*. Oration on the occasion of the acceptance of the chair of Relationship Demographics at the University of Utrecht, 29 October 2003.

this can be found in Chinese adopted children. The story goes that they sometimes spontaneously start eating with chopsticks, although they have never seen it before. Or adopted little boys from South America, living in a feminine family, who might suddenly start exhibiting extreme macho behavior.

In search of dominant views

There are several ways to go in search of dominant views in your own family. In a workshop at Bureau Jeugdzorg Drenthe, participants talked about proverbs typical for their family. The expressions reveal important beliefs and expectations in the family. Some examples:
- *Your home is your castle:* your own family is important.
- *Who is born for a dime, will never be worth a quarter:* whatever you do, you will always be associated with your own kind.
- *One good turn deserves another:* if you are prepared to help someone out, you will also be helped out yourself some time.
- *Don't complain but persevere, and only when you have a fever you can go to bed:* it is important to work hard, not to be lazy.
- *No one gets a program for the concert of life:* difficult things are accepted as they occur.
- *Be yourself, go for what you want yourself:* the individual must be given every opportunity to develop.
- *You can only try your best:* accept that you cannot have everything you want.
- *Never say never:* everything is possible as long as you do your best.

Family story

Family guardian Jannie talks about the great sorrow in her life, her brother's suicide, and how she discovered that this event is linked to family patterns through the generations.

> *"Six years ago, my elder and only brother committed suicide. He had been seriously psychologically ill for as long as I can remember. As a child I didn't know any better. We were so close to each other, so connected to each other, that all my life I could sense the darkness in his head. Although he was older, he looked up to me. I succeeded in everything where he failed, such as relationships, driving license, education, work. But his suffering was my suffering, too. I empathized with him all the way. That burden eventually turned out to be too heavy for me.*
> *When I was eighteen, I was robbed in a supermarket. That's how I ended up with a social worker for victim support. The first two interviews were about the robbery, the remainder of the nine months I saw him were centered on my brother. Whenever I talked about my brother I had to cry, which the social worker pointed out to me. He made me discover that I had two choices. To remain so closely connected and carry the burden of my brother, who was somber and suicidal. Or break the ties and be no longer ill through and for him.*

I talked to my brother, told him that I wanted to distance myself from his illness, because it made me depressed myself. That I did want contact with him, but not when he was in the dark. "I really have to distance myself from you", I said. It was traumatic for him, but he promised to help me and kept his word until his death.

I went on a world trip for a year. During that time, he was doing quite well. But five days before my return he took his own life. Being so sick, he was given permission by my parents. And because he knew that I could never have agreed to his wish, he had to do it before I got back. He was so thin when I saw his lifeless body. I thought dead people always looked so thin, but it turned out that he had lost sixty pounds in my absence.

The protective wraps training made me understand that it's not only my own and my parents' sorrow. The whole family bears the sorrow. My grandfathers, grandmothers, uncles, aunts, cousins, nieces and nephews, too. And not only because of my brother. Many people in the family are genetically affected by psychiatric syndromes. Problem behavior, depression and the threat of suicide not only affects my parents and myself. It is a shared theme, which is an important insight. My father and his four brothers always see to it that calm prevails whenever someone is in danger of going off the rails. There is mediation, problems are solved, a plan of action is drawn up. And no judgments are made. I now have two children of my own, and also for their sake I wanted to know more about my roots, the lives of the generations before me. One evening I had dinner with my mother, my father and my paternal grandmother, and we started to talk about history. My grandmother said that she came from a family with seven children in a small village in the province of Groningen. Her mother was badly abused by her husband, to such an extent that none of the children wanted to sleep on the outside of the box bed, because that meant that you had to be closest to the arguments and the violence, and you might have to take a whack yourself. One day, when my grandmother was still small, her mother left with the seven children, without taking anything else with her. She moved in with her sister in the same village. The income disappeared with the breadwinner, so right away there was extreme poverty. And it was a scandal of such massive proportions, that she and her children were shunned by everyone. My grandmother was no longer allowed to visit her friends. This gave me a better understanding of the reason why my grandmother had developed such a cold, hard side in her life. It also made me see the connection between her mother's rigorous decision to choose her own well-being and happiness, and my similar choice to cut the link with my brother's disease. To my surprise, my great-grandmother's date of death turned out to be the same as my brother's date of birth.

When my grandmother was sixteen, she met my grandfather. He was the brother of her boyfriend, who had died suddenly. My grandfather comforted her and she soon became pregnant, so they got married. Before the age of 24 she had given birth to her five sons, including my father.

My grandfather is from the province of Friesland and he, too, has an emotionally charged history. His father was taken to a concentration camp during the war, and died there. Grandfather grew up in a family of strict Jehovah's Witnesses, but as a result of what happened to his father, he lost all faith in God. Therefore, religion was taboo in our family, although we were imbibed with norms such as respect, and *accepting people as they are. Like my grandmother, my grandfather was a tough person. I remember him as a tall, strict Frisian with a stern expression.*

Both my grandfather and my grandmother lost their father at a young age. Both suffered great losses, which led to bitterness. Contact with them was therefore not always easy. It wasn't until I started college that something changed. I once said to my grandmother that I had a tendency to snap at people in times of stress. "You got that from me!" she said. Then she expressed her appreciation for who I am and what I do. That if she had been given the chance, she would have wanted to live my life. Since then I discuss everything with her. She has become my guide in small and larger existential questions, difficult decisions. A few years ago, my parents went with my grandfather to the camp where his father died. He brought flowers there. The trauma that had marked and colored his life diminished after that. That final farewell calmed him down. He had come to terms with it, my grandmother said. My grandfather has since passed away.

I realize that once my grandmother has gone, too, an entire generation will have disappeared, and a tangible piece of my roots will disappear with it. Today I can still pass on all her stories and her wisdom to my children. When I see how my son and she are connected: nothing comes between them, it's a pure blood tie. My son with his red hair, of which I only recently discovered where it comes from: that there are redheads in the family is because my father's line descends from the red-haired Jews from Germany. Another story, another piece of the puzzle. I consider the stories a gift to my children. Because history is stored in your DNA, your ancestors' blood flows through your veins. It is important to absorb all that family wisdom and to become a better person because of it. "

Family as a protective system

Adopted children are completely cut off from their bloodline, so things often go wrong. Too many adopted children go totally off the rails, find themselves in an identity crisis. What also happens is that black children are placed in a white foster home, and that those children develop identity problems in terms of color. Shamanistic persuasions speak of soul loss. That happens when you don't have access to your blood relatives, your bloodstreams. When you are cut off from a particular family branch, you don't have that wisdom at your disposal. You have no access to the womb of your soul. So, you lose your soul.

The word adoption in itself conceals that the children involved must deal with a number of major events in their lives.[28] In the first place, adopted children have gone through migration, and they often come from countries with a totally different climate, a different culture, language, color, history and organization. However small they may be, they carry this with them. Secondly, adoption always involves the experience of a custodial placement. And thirdly, they usually end up in a

---

28   Tjin A Djie, K. en I. Zwaan (2012), 'Beschermjassen als baken voor intercultureel werken, Mobiliseren van de eigen oplossingsstrategieën van familiesystemen'. In: M. Berk, K. Verhaar, A. Hoogenboom e.a. (eds.), *De jeugdprofessional in ontwikkeling*. Kluwer.

family with a mother who carries the loss experience of unwanted childlessness. This can turn them into second generation traumatized children, like children of war victims and children of migrants, who also often carry the losses their parents have experienced. Consequently, adopted children almost always suffer from accumulated loss, which can lead to identity problems if it goes unnoticed and isn't recognized.

Over the years, several care workers at Bureau Jeugdzorg Drenthe discovered that children who were placed in a family with a completely different background compared to where they came from, virtually always went off the rails. For example, behavioral scientist Gré. She herself grew up in a disadvantaged neighborhood:

> *I started off as a family guardian and I noticed that, on the basis of my own background, it was very easy for me to identify with problem families from disadvantaged areas. It was one hundred per cent recognition. I recognized the feeling those people had, of being worthless. That feeling I have often had myself. So you know that you have to communicate in a different way, and that you shouldn't have great expectations. That you shouldn't impose your norms and values. Which is exactly what I often saw happening in family guardianship. Children being taken into care because the parents can't handle them. And then placing them in a foster family with a totally different background. I was fiercely opposed to this. What's the point in that!? All right, it's not very clean there. So what! In the team they would say: 'You can't leave those children with those parents.' 'Why not?', I would say. 'Come on! I've seen that those parents love those kids! You put them in a foster home. And then what?' That was the reason for me to eventually leave the family guardianship sector.*

It is important for children to know where they come from and to maintain ties with their background, to know the stories. Knowing where you come from leads to a strong identity and gives you a foundation to move through life. Families are by definition the best context for children to grow up in. Families should be given the assignment to take care of their children themselves. And no outsider should be the one to judge whether any particular member of the family is the best option for the child, because the family itself knows best. You must trust the family to be able to judge for itself which member of the family is best suited to take care of the child once the parents are no longer available as providers of care. The figures of authority in the system will play an important role in this. As a care worker, you can try and find these figures of authority in order to facilitate the process. But families should never be disqualified from the strengths they carry within them. If it is not possible for the child to live with its own parents, then the first choice should be the grandparents or an aunt or uncle.

Foster families or adoptive families are a good alternative if there is really no possibility within the children's own family. Provided the family gives permission, the children are not cut off from their roots, and are housed in a system similar to the one they come from.

Destructive family patterns

Rituals and traditions such as female circumcision and honor killings are mechanisms that aim to guarantee the survival of the family. They are often rites of passage, marking important life phase transitions. Circumcision is the initiation ritual for girls who reach childbearing age. And honor killings 'cleanse' shameful events in the family. It is a way of giving shape to family continuity. Originally, these patterns ensured bonds in families, it held them together, provided absorption and embedment in the we-oriented system. They once had a constructive function, and it is important to go back to the value they used to have in order to be able to change them. What was their original meaning, and what caused the descent into a destructive pattern?

It's often the older women who carry and perpetuate the traditions, and who feel under enormous threat once different ideas come up. If you reconnect people to their core values, their original views, then the necessary security and space are created to keep the conversation going. The traditions were originally meant to ensure continuation, but due to changes and in today's context, they have the opposite effect and lead to break-ups and loss. Instead of a one-to-one rejection of these rituals, it would be preferable for care workers to enter into discussions with the family about the meaning of the patterns.

We have seen that each family has its figures of authority, those responsible for the important decisions in the family. At the same time, there are often family members who have acquired authority by disrupting certain patterns. They have introduced innovation, and if they have been successful in doing so, this has conferred on them a certain position. Think of the uncle who was the first to go to university, the cousin who emigrated to make a better life for himself, or the aunt who started a successful business of her own and did very well. The people who gained respect by doing something completely different are also those who can help to break through the destructive patterns, to redirect those patterns. In conversation with the traditional figures of authority, they can look for ways to find new rituals which will ensure continuation of the old values. If the initiative for change is taken in the family itself, this will offer the best prospects for an effective and supported result. That is where the strength of families lies.[29]

Finally

This chapter was about families: collective-oriented families and individual-oriented families. Apparently there are many similarities. The strengths of the extended family in we-oriented systems are often denied in I-oriented systems, but there too they are latent. It is important to utilize these strengths not only among migrants, but also among native Dutch families. The next chapter is about migration and its impact on families. Migrants commute between multiple cultures, multiple

---

29 Tjin A Djie, K. en I. Zwaan (2013), 'Beschermjassen: het zelfoplossend vermogen van families', *Tijdschrift Kinder- & Jeugdpsychotherapie* 40, nr. 4.

contexts. Migration carries trauma with it, and tends to disrupt family continuity. Having knowledge and insight in aspects of migration helps to provide migrants with adequate care.

Assignment

- How is your family organized?
- Do you belong to a predominantly I-oriented system or a we-oriented system?
- What views, aphorisms and sacred cows exist?
- Who belongs to the dominant group guarding these views?
- How are decisions made?
- Who are the ones to disrupt things?
- How is the relationship with the disruptors maintained?
- What do you know about your fellow students, colleagues or clients with regard to these questions? Please give some examples.

5

Impact of migration

Kitlyn: "I really hate going to Suriname. I don't understand the codes. I feel like a stranger in my own country. So throughout my stay, I'm waiting for the plane to take me back. At the same time, there's something you can do with that old world and the new world, create something new out of it. That's the power of migration."

Kitlyn emigrated to the Netherlands when she was 15. Three elder sisters preceded her, and her two younger sisters followed later. In her family, emigrating felt like just going up a flight of stairs and then you lived in the Netherlands. It was taken for granted. Many migrants don't realize the impact of migration. They think it's like taking the bus to go around the corner. Nothing special, nothing to worry about. Life resumes, it just goes on. But of course that's not the way it is. If people develop anxiety complaints or other psychological problems later on, this often goes back to the migration. Research has shown that migration is a major risk factor for schizophrenia. Increased numbers of both first-generation and second-generation migrants show that this is not a biological matter. Social factors associated with migration increase the chances of the disease.[1] Hence, migration drastically affects someone's emotional system. Migrants themselves often don't realize this. It's a blind spot.

An important theme for migrants from we-oriented systems is how migration affects family continuity. If you're used to functioning in a three-generation or four-generation family, migration will lead to major disruption. Because how can you consult with the figures of authority whenever important decisions are to be made? How can you keep contributing to the family assignment? And how can you continue to enjoy protection from your family when they're not around? A Dutch nuclear family will run into such problems less frequently following migration. Because Dutch people grew up with different ideas about family. The nuclear family takes care of itself and will therefore continue to function after migration. The Dutch, therefore, have a blind spot for the impact of migration on migrants coming from a we-oriented system.

In addition, coming from a culture of singular thinking, the Dutch have difficulty dealing with cultural diversity. Dominant views in the Netherlands about the psychological value of children, the value attached to autonomy and other typically Dutch values, are unconsciously regarded as superior. That is why migrants are often not understood, and why there is no room for the cultural identity of migrants within the Dutch context. For many migrants, this leads to an isolated experience of their own culture, without the possibility to link this to Dutch cultural views. Whereas that is precisely where the opportunities lie in a multicultural society.

This chapter is about migration. First of all, it is explained why migration should be regarded as an important life phase transition. Next, the importance of language with regard to migration is examined. The effect of migration on family continuity is highlighted. The different effects of migration on the different generations are described. The affronts experienced by migrants will be looked at, as well as the effects of these affronts. Finally, attention is paid to examples of how to combine the best of both worlds and how the so-called transitional space offers a place to connect here with there.

---

[1] Selten, J.P. (2002), 'Epidemiologie van schizofrenie bij migranten in Nederland', *Tijdschrift voor psychiatrie* 44-10, pp. 665-675.

Migration is a special life phase transition

A life phase transition is a period in your life in which you pass from one situation to a new situation. Important life phase transitions include the transition from teenage years to adolescence, changing jobs, having a child, or the death of a loved one. A characteristic feature of a life phase transition is uncertainty. You have to reinvent yourself to proceed to the next phase.[2]

Migration to a different country, a different culture, constitutes a major change in someone's life. It's not just any move. You leave your extended family, your language, your environment, your culture. Migration is a complex transition, because a great many changes occur simultaneously. The anthropological term *liminality* offers a concept to gain insight into the transition from one phase to another.[3] The liminal phase is the phase in which you leave the old behind and have not yet embraced the new. You are, as it were, between two worlds. In the case of migration, it represents the transition from one culture to another. It is a vulnerable and stressful period, that is even more difficult when migration is accompanied by violence and war trauma, as is the case with many refugees. Also, when the migrant is of a vulnerable age, such as puberty, or when there is discrimination in the new country, this will make the transition more difficult. The vulnerability entailed by migration is intensified in such cases.

The liminal phase is not only a vulnerable phase, it also offers room for creativity. Because there is nothing at all in this phase, you can create something new out of what was and what will be. Connect the past with the present. There is always loss as well as enrichment in this phase.[4] This is sometimes referred to as the transitional space. More about that later in this chapter.

Migration is a special life phase transition. With each new life phase transition, the migration experience presents itself afresh. In the vulnerable period of a life phase transition, such as the loss of a parent, a migrant will always be confronted again with the experience of loss that the migration entailed. This is called a layered life phase transition. Experiences of loss accumulate. For that reason, migrants are all the more vulnerable when it comes to life phase transitions. Trauma, too, is a special life phase transition that reasserts itself with every transition. Migrants with traumatic experiences, such as many refugees, often report to healthcare authorities with seemingly psychiatric complaints. This often involves three or four life phase transitions that manifest themselves simultaneously.

It is important to provide migrants who find themselves in a layered life phase transition with 'protective wraps'. As we saw before, this term is based on the notion

---

2 Groeneveld, L., 'Voel je senang in een beschermjas', interview with K. Tjin A Djie in *Contrast*, maart 2007.
3 Bekkum, D. van, M. van de Ende, S. Heezen en A. Hijmans van den Bergh (1996), '"Migratie als Transitie" De liminele kwetsbaarheid van migranten en vluchtelingen'. In: J. de Jong en M. v.d. Berg (eds.), *Handboek Transculturele Psychiatrie en Psychotherapie*. Lisse.
4 Boedjarath, I. en D. van Bekkum (eds.) (1997), *Een blik in de transculturele hulpverlening, 15 jaar ervaring met verlies en verrijking*. Utrecht: Van Arkel.

of 'enveloppement' from French transcultural system therapy.[5] By immersing people in the group or culture from which they have come, they will be able to compose themselves. They will be revitalized and will come up with solutions for their situation. It's a matter of very basic things, such as photos from the past, food, language or culture.

Language

In the Netherlands, twice as many migrant women as Dutch women die in childbirth. In part this is due to their needs during labor not being understood. And not only as regards perception. People can also literally lose their second language on such an occasion. A Dutch woman said that she could no longer speak a word of German during her delivery, even though at the time she had been living in Germany for six years. So, the shock caused by the experience can make people suddenly lose a language they formerly had at their disposal.

In chapter 3 we saw that language is an important aspect of cultural identity. Language is culture, language is identity. The easiest way to show your love for your child is in your first language. You sing lullabies in your first language. The best way of showing your feelings is in your own language. Language carries ideas. The positioning of *I* for example. In Dutch, it's always at the front, while in Turkish it's always at the end of the sentence. That's in line with the ideas of the Turkish we-culture and the Dutch I-culture. Switching between languages means being loyal to different ideas. And loss of language means loss of culture, loss of identity.

It is important that migrant children are raised bilingually, that they not only learn Dutch. In the province of Friesland, for example, the two-language policy (Frisian and standard Dutch) has worked very well. But the Dutch tendency towards linear, unambiguous thinking leaves little room for bilingualism among migrants, while it is extremely important for second-generation and third-generation migrants to be able to talk to their parents in their mother tongue. Because, with the loss of their own language, children of migrants lose the connection with their culture and with their parents. If you don't speak the language of your parents, you don't understand the ideas implied in it. This creates identity problems. There is also the risk of the parents losing their understanding of Dutch as they get older. Since, in a layered life phase transition such as getting old when one has a migration history, it is easy to lose one's second language.

Case manager Cees:

> *"During Kitlyn's training sessions it became clear to me that my children have an adaptation process similar to that of migrants in the Netherlands. My youngest lived in Spain at the time, my eldest in Sweden. Thijs and Astrid have decided to raise their child, my granddaughter, bilingually. This means that she speaks Swedish, while he very*

---

5   Sterman, D. (1996), Een olijfboom op de ijsberg. *Een transcultureel-psychiatrische visie op en behandeling van jonge Noord-Afrikanen en hun families*. Nederlands Centrum Buitenlanders; republished by door Pharos (2007).

consistently speaks Dutch to her. When she is with us we speak Dutch, just to see how it works. Astrid's family lives near them, which means they are more prominent in her life. And in a while, she will be going to a Swedish school. So Swedish will become her main language. But the idea behind teaching her to speak Dutch as well is that it will be nice if later on she can understand us, and that it will be no problem for us to communicate with her as she gets older. We speak English with Astrid. My son himself didn't actually see the need for his daughter to learn Dutch, but Astrid was very determined. That's the way it had to be done! Perhaps it has to do with taking into account the fact that we're getting older. Knowledge of foreign languages can fade with age, or so I've heard. But if she speaks Dutch, we can still communicate with her, even when we're 88! I think it's important that my granddaughter learns something about the Dutch background and culture. She will be growing up in Sweden, so she will take her being Swedish for granted. But I think that, if at a certain age she gets curious about the Dutch part, then it will be nice if we can talk about that. I myself grew up in a family where my father's parents were very important. They didn't live nearby. But every summer we went on holiday to The Hague, where they lived. Although I must say there were also economic reasons for it, because at the time my father didn't make much money. There was a close relationship. As a matter of fact, we went through a lot together. I, too, would like to mean a lot to my grandchildren. I don't yet know how to meet that need in a practical way. But we have decided to buy a small house in Sweden if possible, so that we've got a spot there and can stay a little longer. "

Effect of migration on family continuity

We have seen that family continuity is a major asset in collective systems. Members of a family across three or even four generations are jointly responsible for ensuring continuity. There is always a division of tasks: every extended family has figures of authority who are called upon when discontinuity threatens. Hence, migration radically affects family life. After migration, the decision-making process must instantly be dealt with in a different way. Moreover, in the new context there is a substantial lack of understanding for the causes of the discontinuity. Take, for example, arranged marriages. If a North African girl in the Netherlands suddenly starts looking at a different man from the one to whom she has been coupled by the family, three or four generations would in principle have to intervene in order to rectify this. Among Dutch people this evokes a great deal of incomprehension, because it touches on the ideal of children's autonomy. Dutch care workers wonder what this grandfather has to do with it. And the family itself agonizes over how to shape the decision-making in order to arrive at a solution. All those generations are put under great pressure to ensure continuation of that process.

The story of intercultural project member Jeanne shows how after migration an appeal can be made to figures of authority in an extended family.

" *A couple of weeks ago, I received a call from a Rwandan client. She said that she was suffering from psychosis and was worried about her children. She is divorced from her husband, who also lives in the Netherlands. From time to time he takes care of the*

> children, but he is very unreliable. When I was with her, she telephoned her ex and begged him to come and take care of her children. But he didn't come, he made up all kinds of excuses why it wasn't possible. The children could temporarily be put up with a neighbor, but the problem was that they had to be housed somewhere for a longer period of time, so that the mother could work on her healing process. Only the father could take care of the children. As Bureau Jeugdzorg Drenthe, we had to stay involved as long as this wasn't settled. When later on I was with her again, I saw that her ex-husband was there. It emerged that she had called her in-laws in Rwanda. There is an aunt there for whom he feels much respect and admiration. That particular aunt turned out to have called him immediately after the woman's telephone call. She gave him an earful, said that despite the divorce he remains responsible for the children, and therefore has to take care of them when his ex-wife is ill. The mother had previously told me that she was terribly lonely. That she had nobody here to advise her about herself or her children. She missed wise people around her like she had in Rwanda, that's the way she said it. I then made a genogram, a family drawing, with her. From that it appeared that she still had a good relationship with her former in-laws. And that she telephoned them from time to time. Perhaps that helped her in getting the idea to call that aunt."

Many migrants experience the obligation to financially support their families in their home country as a burden. In general, migrants did not come here because of their individual dream, but because of the family's dream. To make that dream come true is an arduous task, in which they often don't succeed. You sometimes see migrants standing next to a nice big car to have their picture taken. They send that picture home, to show that they're making out all right. Their own failure is the failure to contribute to family continuity.

Child psychiatrist Sita Somers gave the following example:

> "A Turkish family had been torn apart for three generations. Through marriages with cousins they tried to keep the family together, but time and again this had failed. Research showed that in the past the family had been politically divided: one part supported the Western-oriented movement, while the other part was conservative. The split led to disruption in every generation. In the fourth generation it even led to addiction problems. Initially, the family was unable to appoint mediators. Nevertheless, the mother subsequently asked me to sign a letter for Social Affairs to get permission for a stay in Turkey. I grasped what was going to happen and signed. And sure enough, after she returned it emerged that several great-uncles had been consulted in order to find solutions and make decisions regarding the problem situation. Ergo, after strong insistence on my part – which is a (virtually) standard necessity in cases of families with multiple ruptures – the self-healing capacity was set in motion again."[6]

---

6   Somers, S., K. Tjin A Djie en I. Zwaan (2012), 'De therapeut als edelsmid'. In: Y. te Poel et al. (ed.), *Interculturele diagnostiek bij kinderen en jongeren*. NIP & NVO.

Different generations

Generalizing is of course 'not done', but we can speculate somewhat about the causes of whether or not migrants feel at home in the Netherlands. Whether or not migrants have started to feel at home here depends to a large extent on the relationship of the Netherlands with the country of origin. Many Surinamese and Antilleans still consider Beatrix their queen. Moreover, they speak almost the same language as the Dutch. Surinamese have close ties to the Netherlands. Surinamese in the Netherlands generally do well. Antilleans have a different language from the Dutch. They are more resistant to speaking Dutch. For them, Dutch is the language of the oppressor. 90% of Moroccans in the Netherlands are Berbers. And Berbers are an oppressed people in Morocco itself. Oppressed by the Arabs for the past 1000 years and subsequently by the French in the colonial era. So, in the Netherlands they experience a threefold oppression, as it were. As a result, they are often suspicious and distrustful. Turkey was never colonized. Turkish people in the Netherlands display completely different behavior and do not feel submissive. They do, however, feel aggrieved, because they are viewed and approached as a minority, while they have never been conquered as a people.

There are also differences between generations of migrants. The first generation of migrants can be seen to tightly hold on to their old culture. When you enter their houses, it's like stepping into the world of the home country. The interior, the cookies, the food. The people seem to be frozen. The culture stops developing from the moment of migration. Painful feelings surrounding migration are made bearable because it was decided beforehand by both the migrant and the family that the migration was temporary.[7] They will eventually return to the home country. Hence, there is no need to embrace the new living environment. This is the reason why many families have never really come to terms with the migration. And while the clock of the migrant in the Netherlands has stopped, the culture in the home country continues to develop. This leads to a sense of no longer belonging anywhere. People feel like strangers there as well as here. The second generation does not feel the loss of culture, country and family. But they do feel the pain of the first generation. And to spare their parents, they don't talk about it, don't ask about it. They don't want to stir up that grief. But because of this, no exchange takes place about a very essential part of family history. Parents don't want to burden their children with it and children want to protect their parents from pain. While there is a great sense of disruption among the parents. The children inherit all kinds of beliefs and cultural values that are really only appropriate in the home country. Because of school and friends, they undergo more and more Western influences, giving rise to loyalty conflicts and questions about their migration history. It's a subject you often come across in the care sector. In such cases, it is necessary to let that connection flow again by unraveling such issues and encouraging exchange with the parents about them. The interconnectedness with the old culture is

---

[7] Meurs, P. en A. Gailly (1999), *Wortelen in andere aarde, Migrantengezinnen en hulpverleners ontmoeten cultuurverschil*. Leuven/Amersfoort: Acco.

important to make it easier to cope with the encounter with the new culture.[8] The third generation should be able to play with the different views within the generations.

Intercultural project member Jeanne tells how her children discover their roots in Suriname.

> **"** In the 1950s, my parents came to the Netherlands from Suriname. I am the youngest of eight children, and the only one born here. My parents acted as a kind of foster family for Surinamese children who were sent to the Netherlands with a view to their future. I inherited a Surinamese part, but was reared here. At around 18, I sort of went in search of my roots. At the Social Academy, I deliberately opted for an internship in a Surinamese institution. You know, you just miss a piece of Suriname, because you weren't born there. In 1980, I got married to a Dutch man. With him I visited Suriname, together with my mother, my father and other members of the family. There, things started to fall into place. When I got back, I started working for the Surinamese foundation right away. I did that for years. After all, when you're looking for your roots, you want to interact with the people who also come from there. At some point I was done with it. I thought this is it, I live in the Netherlands. I have explored that part of my life story and I have found out about it. And in the Netherlands, you cannot keep doing everything from that Surinamese perspective. I changed my job and had three daughters. But I always said to my husband, once the children are grown up we must go back to visit Suriname again. They will have to be at an age when it will be a very conscious experience for them, because it is also a part of their culture.
> Last year finally the time had come. The youngest had turned 18. I said, now you're no longer children and as grown-ups you will visit my country. And your country. The middle one started muttering. She didn't want to go. There are beasts there, they have this and that. But as the date approached, she started to read more and more and she became more and more enthusiastic. When we arrived in Suriname, I saw things happening to the children. Especially to the youngest. At times she can be a bit obstinate. And there she actually became the child who most frequently took the initiative, who made contact with people.
> My brother is divorced. He lives in Suriname and has two sons in their twenties. He and his children had fallen out with each other. He hadn't seen them in a year. But my children wanted to see those boys. It's family, they said. But, my brother says, they don't want to come, we have no contact. So, my youngest picks up the phone and calls them. We're here and I'll kick you if you don't come! It's true! And those boys, they came. My brother said that what those girls had managed to do I could never have done myself. The contact with him was restored. Initially, the boys were a bit awkward, but the girls were all over those boys right away. They didn't want to shake hands, they wanted a real Surinamese brasa, a real hug. Their cousins never got a chance to withdraw. After that, they went along everywhere. Also to visit other members of the family, whom they themselves hardly ever saw anymore. Those girls have had a binding effect on the whole

---

8   Meurs, P. en A. Gailly (1999), *Wortelen in andere aarde, Migrantengezinnen en hulpverleners ontmoeten cultuurverschil*. Leuven/Amersfoort: Acco.

family there. And they still have daily email contact with their cousins.
I noticed something happening to my children. They became more and more Surinamese. They felt really good about themselves, were also looking very well. Radiant, you can still see that when you look at the pictures. And not only because they had such a good time, but also because they met the family. Everyone welcomed them, they were immediately accepted. Like, oh, those are Jeanne's children. Whereas their Dutch side, they're very loosely connected. But here it felt like a warm bath to them. They said, mum, they don't even know who we are! No, I would say, the fact that you're my children is enough.
Two of my children are now saving to go back for Christmas. The profile they have created on the internet says that they were born in Suriname, Paramaribo. They've bought a Surinamese flag, because after the youngest has passed her final exams, the Surinamese flag must fly. They also have Surinamese style pants and purses. I think that these days if you were to call them Dutch, they would be seriously offended, whereas before that was just the way it was. No matter how you look at it, you're a child of Suriname. And I think that the children sensed that when we were there. **"**

Commuting

Migrants must be loyal to the views of the family, or of the culture of origin. But they must also become loyal to the views of the Netherlands. Sometimes these things cannot be reconciled. If you act in a certain way towards your children and in a different way towards your mother, and then suddenly they are together, that can be extremely tiring. Migrants must be loyal to one person and loyal to another. As long as the contexts are separated, this is not very difficult. If, for example, at school you call out: "That stupid Islam!" and at home you say: "Those stupid Dutch!", then that's quite easy to maintain. But when they are suddenly together in a room, it can get very complicated. Commuting between contexts means that you must be able to be loyal to views that are sometimes conflicting. The second generation in particular has to deal with this. Dutch people often cannot comprehend this. It is interpreted as being ambiguous, saying something different from day to day. The Dutch believe that you should be the same everywhere, and always say the same. This norm is hardly ever questioned. And yet this is not always the case for the Dutch either. Because the loyalty you feel as a mother requires different statements than your loyalty as a career woman or your loyalty as a lover. Hence, native Dutch people, too, constantly commute between all kinds of contexts.

Affronts

The first generation of migrant workers frequently doesn't speak the Dutch language. So they don't hear what is being said about them, and suffer less from affronts. While the second generation is constantly confronted with remarks like 'go back to your own country'. Affronts are context-related. When Kitlyn walks down the street with her husband in Suriname, people will think that she's carrying on with a tourist. As a passer-by, you can ignore that kind of thing. When you live somewhere, it's more difficult.

Kitlyn:

> "One of my sons has friends who are very dear to him. They say, all those negroes in town, we don't want to have anything to do with them. This makes my son feel like he's being knocked back and forth, like a ping-pong ball. What should I do? Should I hit them? After all, I'm a negro too. If he doesn't speak out, it will keep nagging him. Do I still want to hang out with them or not?"

The reason for much of the hurt is that the position and status you had in your home country have disappeared after migration. This has a lot to do with the fact that for centuries, the Netherlands has been in a superior position as the colonizer and as a rich country. Due to the impact of the war, Germany has achieved self-reflection and has a very different attitude towards migrants. But in the Netherlands, migrants still get the message that they are inferior.

Kitlyn:

> "A friend of mine is a millionaire in Suriname. Her son is studying here and started dating a Dutch girl. The girl's family made it clear that they didn't think this was a good idea, their daughter with a Surinamese boy. They broke up. The boy could never have imagined not being good enough for anyone. In Suriname every girl wants him, because he is the son of a millionaire."

Identity is very context-related. Many refugees are highly educated, that is why they had the means to come to the Netherlands. But here, they're no longer worth anything. Here, their capacities are not visible, they don't get any appreciation for who they are, for who they were in the home country. That hurts. It also leads to crisis within the family. In her work, Kitlyn met an Iranian refugee. Her daughter had been born in the Netherlands. She only knew her mother as a marginalized refugee in a society that didn't need her. "When I'm in Iran, I'm the queen in my family. I would very much like to show her that. Because I will never be able to show her that, she has a distorted image of me, she doesn't know who I really am." Her daughter had threatened and verbally abused her. The mother was convinced that if she could present herself the way she was in her home country, the daughter wouldn't dream of behaving like that. Eventually, circumstances and the political climate made it possible to travel to Iran with the child. It had an amazing effect. The daughter met the grandmother. She saw her uncles bow to her mother, she saw her mother as the queen in that family. She has stopped threatening and using abusive language. As a result of the journey, the relationship between mother and daughter was healed. Class, income disparities and ethnicity are characteristics on the basis of which people are included and excluded. These characteristics vary per country, per group and per context.⁹ Inclusion and exclusion mechanisms are at work always and everywhere. This doesn't have to be a bad thing in itself, as it also offers protection for the survival of your own group. But if it is meant to be condescending and stigmatizing, exclusion can lead to discrimination, sexism and racism. The effect of being affronted is often that the original culture becomes a shelter to hide in and to be cultivated. A breeding ground for segregation and fundamentalism. But if migrants were to be welcomed in their new environment and allowed to feel at home, then the home country and the original culture could be used as a primal source from which to draw strength and revitalization.

Protective wraps in the transitional space

In developmental psychology, the term transition indicates a space where children can cope with the absence of their mother.[10] With the aid of a familiar object, such as a toy, they find the security within themselves to be alone for a little while. In a world where, due to migration or loss of family awareness, people find less and less security in their living environment, it is important to look for anchors to help them to be at home within themselves. To be able to cope with the lack of safe embedment. For migrants, the transitional space is a vulnerable in-between space, where they have to reinvent themselves. They need to think about how to deal with the old and the new loyalties. To reflect on what was and what is to come. And with whom to talk about that. Perhaps it's best with someone coming from neither the old nor the new context. To ensure a successful transition, it is important to feel secure. And for that, protective wraps are needed.[11]

Kitlyn once talked to two Afghan brothers who, together with two other underage asylum seekers, were living in a relief center. During their flight, one of the brothers had incurred a leg injury. They had been in the Netherlands for a year, and the wound just wouldn't heal. There was a lot of concern about that. 'What did you bring from home to keep you going here?' Kitlyn asked. They were surprised: no one had ever asked them such a question before. They immediately told her that their mother had given them a page from the Quran to take with them, with a holder for the piece of paper and a cloth to put it on. Before their enforced departure, she had urged her sons to read that page to each other once a day. Kitlyn asked: 'What was the thought behind that?' To which one of the boys replied: 'For us to stick together.'[12]

---

9   Gowricharn, R. (2001), 'In- en uitsluiting in Nederland. Een overzicht van empirische bevindingen'; study Wetenschappelijke Raad voor het Regeringsbeleid, Rijswijk.
10 Winnicott, D. (1953), 'Transitional objects and transitional phenomena', Int. J. Psychoanal., 34:89-97.
11 Bekkum, D. van, G.O. Helberg, K. Tjin A Djie en I. Zwaan (2010), 'Rituelen en beschermjassen'. In: J. de Jong en S. Colijn (eds.), Handboek culturele psychiatrie en psychotherapie. Utrecht: De Tijdstroom.
12 Tjin A Djie, K. en I. Zwaan (2015), Beschermjassen op school, aandacht voor verschil in het onderwijs. Assen: Koninklijke van Gorcum

The best of both worlds

Van Bekkum: "A small number of migrants doesn't manage to make it through the unsettling transition. These migrants get stuck between two worlds. They become psychologically unbalanced and initially seek help in their own circle." This is mainly a result of the inadequate two-way interaction. Migrants are primarily expected to make an effort when it comes to integration. But integration is not really possible without a contribution from the native Dutch. The norm for migrants in the Netherlands is to fully embrace Dutch culture and the Dutch language. This ethnocentric view is a major stumbling block for integration and hence for multicultural society. Ethnocentrism means taking your own culture as the benchmark for judging other cultures. The lenses through which you look show a world that measures up to your own cultural norms and values.[13] In order to achieve successful integration, it is important that migrants anchor interconnectedness within their original culture. In a country that conveys the message that the dominant culture is the better one, it is difficult to connect original and new cultural perspectives.[14]

Halleh Ghorashi[15] compared the way in which Iranian women in North America and in the Netherlands settled into the new society. She likewise concludes that there should be room for differences in a multicultural society. Her research shows that Iranian women in the Netherlands found it very difficult to enter into an emotional bond with the Netherlands, whereas Iranian women in America succeeded in that respect. She found out that Iranians in the Southern California city of Irvine celebrate the Mehregan annual fall festival. This is a celebration from Persian ancient history, which today is no longer celebrated anywhere in Iran. On the one hand, this festival provides the Iranians with a sense of home, paying homage to their own old traditions. On the other hand, it ensures a connection with America, because it is comparable to Thanksgiving. The American identity is based on freedom and democracy. America is the country of migration. This offers room for cultural individuality and makes it possible for migrants to feel at home. In the Netherlands, however, 'well-integrated' Iranian women were unable to appropriate the Dutch identity. They feel excluded and not regarded as equals. According to Ghorashi, this is due to the way in which the Dutch approach integration. You either adapt or you go back home. This always assumes strong ties with the home country, and that people either go back there or let go of those ties. The Dutch identity is, in exaggerated terms, white and Christian. It is impossible for Iranians to adopt those traits. Integration in accordance with the Dutch norm is not feasible. Ghorashi: "Even migrants who were born and bred here often have the feeling that they have no access to the hidden codes of Dutch identity. What it comes down to is that the

---

13 Bekkum, D. van (2004), 'Nederlandse identiteit als basis voor burgerschap – een antropologische visie', Civis Mundi, January.
14 Meurs, P. en A. Gailly (1999), *Wortelen in andere aarde, Migrantengezinnen en hulpverleners ontmoeten cultuurverschil.* Leuven/Amersfoort: Acco.
15 Ghorashi, H., 'Is de tijd rijp voor reflectie op integratievraagstukken?' *D66 tijdschrift Thema Idee*, September 2006.

Dutch identity does not allow for diversity, but also that migrants cannot connect with this identity."

Finally

It is important to pay attention to the impact of migration on migrants. We should also provide scope for migrants to connect parts of their original culture to the Dutch identity. As a care worker, together with your client you can look for important anchors and protective wraps from the past that can help to provide confidence and security in the here and now. Now that we have some knowledge about aspects of diversity, families and migration, it's time to turn to practice. How can you as a person gain more understanding, connect more closely with the Other? That is what the next chapter is about. Chapter 6 deals with intercultural competencies. The knowledge and skills you need to enter into a dialogue with your fellow (wo)man.

Assignment

- What major life phase transitions have you and your family experienced? Think also of earlier generations. What impact does this have on your or your family's life?
- Give an example of a case in which you apply the theory of this chapter.

6

Intercultural competencies

Kitlyn: "A friend of my youngest son did less well at swimming lessons. His mother said to me: 'I suppose you go swimming with him every week, for him to be doing so well?'. I said: 'No, he's just got good hand-leg coordination or something, I don't know.' But even so she still didn't understand why my son was better at swimming than hers. She sought the solution in my endeavors, I sought it in his swimming talent. We each spoke a different language."

The fact that it is very difficult to get the dialogue with 'the Other' off the ground and to keep it open, becomes apparent by the shockingly high divorce rate among bicultural couples. 17% of native Dutch marriages is dissolved within ten years. For marriages between a native Dutch woman and a migrant man, that percentage is three times as high, namely 50%.[1] Mixed marriages that succeed, apparently employ certain strategies. On the one hand, there is a considerable degree of acceptance of the partner's culture and on the other hand, discussion of complicated and painful themes is avoided. Hondius concludes from the successful relation strategies among bicultural partners that traits such as patience, prudence, restraint and determination might also in society contribute to tolerance and the acceptance of ethnic and religious differences.[2]

The model for intercultural competencies[3] provides tools to increase the chances of an open dialogue with someone from a different culture or with a different background from yours. This model consists of a number of elements. First of all, it is important to have some knowledge of your own cultural baggage. Your own background plays a very important role in how you act and react in contacts with others. Next, it is important to have knowledge of the other person. What is the migration history, what is the family structure, and other important information. Being aware of your own sacred cows that you encounter in your contact with others is essential. Once you recognize them, you can park them for a while, and communication will remain open. To be able to put yourself in the other person's shoes means that you're able to switch perspectives. It's about empathizing and understanding, for example what it means to be part of a collective system. Or what the impact is of a migration history. You must also assume that there are always hidden dimensions. Those are the blind spots in communication. This chapter deals with the different elements of the model.[4] Subsequently, we will discuss the concepts of empathy and compassion as conditions for intercultural communication. Stories illustrate what this means in practice.

Knowledge of your own cultural baggage

What matters when it comes to knowledge of your own cultural baggage, is that you become aware of everything you take for granted. Because through becoming aware of this, you gain insight into 'the Other' within yourself. You no longer see the things that are always with you. Whereas these can be essential in communicating with people for whom such things are not so obvious. Your own cultural baggage includes knowledge of your own country, history, culture, norms and values, you name it. In addition, the history and the structure of your family are important.

---

1   Huis, M. van en L. Steenhof (2004), 'Echtscheidingskansen van allochtonen in Nederland', *Bevolking en gezin*, 33, 2, pp. 127-154.
2   Hondius, D., 'Gemengde huwelijken, gemengde gevoelens', DEMOS, vol. 19, August 2003.
3   Roth, J. (1996), 'Workshop intercultural concepts 3rd European summer seminar in intercultural studies'.
4   See also Tjin A Djie, K. (2002), 'De bijzondere opdracht van migrantenkinderen'. In: C.J.A. Roosen, A. Savenije, A. Kolman en R. Beunderman (eds.) *'Over een grens', Psychotherapie met adolescenten*, Assen: Koninklijke Van Gorcum.

Because no matter how much you think of yourself as an autonomous being, the messages passed on to you by your family shape you more than you think, as we saw in chapter 4. Someone might make an innocent remark, which touches on a sore spot with you. Because it touches on a part of your family that is about exclusion, discontinuity, losses or conflict, you react violently, while you are not aware of the source of that violence. Once you know where certain ideas come from, you can park them for a while when communicating.

Various exercises may help to uncover your own family story, the messages in your family. The proverbs that are part of your family. Because each family has its own family language, family sayings or proverbs. If a family has appropriated a certain saying, this will often come back in all the generations and in the different family branches. Or where your name stems from.[5] Whether or not you're named after a family member. Whether there's a story to your name. The name is often related to the family context, but also to the village or the province. Naming often follows traditions, in the sense that the eldest son is named after his father's father and the eldest daughter after her mother's mother. Other families may deviate from this. Stories about naming frequently lead to information on the acceptance of partnership, importance of men and women, conflicts, class differences and other interesting facts and views.

The story about the name of youth care worker Pim leads us to his family history.

> *I was born in the Dutch East Indies just after the war. My father's father is Armenian, his mother is Javanese, a native woman. They never got married, but always stayed together. My mother was also born in the Dutch East Indies, as was her father. He was an Indo-European. My mother's mother was born in the Netherlands and descends from the French-Dutch Huguenots. My surname is Apcar, which is an Armenian name. My great-grandfather was an Armenian priest.*
> *He, his wife and their children lived in Isfahan (Iran), where there was a large Armenian community. My great-grandfather later became the head of a church in Singapore. From there, my grandfather ended up on Java as a jobseeker. My father's father got very rich. He owned a cassava plantation and a factory. He extracted flour from the cassava tuber and exported it to America as starch. But the money ran out before my father came of age. Granddad's children were all made to study, and were sent to England and the Netherlands. My father was sent to a Dutch boarding school when he was twelve, and went back when he was about 27. Both of my father's parents died when he was thirteen. My father never had much to say about his background. He came from a large family, he knew his brothers and sisters, and he knew very little else. I got married to a woman who was born and bred in Assen in the province of Drenthe. When my eldest son was born, my wife thought his first name should be Armenian. At that time, we started a correspondence with the only brother of my father who was still alive. We asked him to give us a list of Armenian names, and we wanted to know my grandfather's name. My eldest is named after my grandfather. He was given his second name. Our other son was also given Armenian names. We never managed to*

---

5   Jessurun, C.M. (2010), *Transculturele vaardigheden voor therapeuten*. Bussum: Coutinho.

find out much more. Until a cousin of mine telephoned me in 2001. The son of one of my father's elder sisters. He lives in America, and we visited him. Because he always lived near my grandfather and grandmother, he knows a lot more about my family's background. So, from 2001 onwards we have become more aware of it. We have seen and were given many photographs. I have some things that belonged to my granddad and grandma, jewelry and the like. That cousin of mine had brought those with him when he came from Indonesia as a young adult. Initially he went to the Netherlands, married a Dutch woman and then left for America. He died last year, and we received even more of my grandfather's stuff. At some stage my cousin had invited my father, but my father was 90 at the time and didn't want to risk the journey. That's why we went there instead. My wife saw that we had a lot in common, even though we grew up in different environments, in different cultures really. I think you inherit more family traits than scientists have established so far. Not just the color of your eyes and hair or your character. Behavior is also sometimes similar. My wife saw many similarities in how we talk to each other, how we think, but also in how we prepare our food. After that I started focusing even more on my cultural background. Started to find out more. We spent two and a half weeks with that cousin. He said, I got something for you. He took us to a bank and removed my grandfather's ring from a safe. There were also two bracelets and a pin that had belonged to my grandmother. The real Javanese wear a top knot on their heads and the somewhat richer people had a beautiful golden pin stuck in it. And there was also a wallet that had belonged to my grandfather, with his initials on it. I gave it all to my father. That really touched him. My father owned nothing at all from the past. He became more aware of it. He never used to talk about it, but from then on we started talking more. The fact that we decided to name my eldest son after my grandfather also meant a lot to my father. **"**

For yourself it's sometimes a good thing to transform a family assignment that's in your way. If the message is 'who is born for a dime, will never be worth a quarter' you could remain stuck for life in the social environment you've come from. Even though you're trying to rise above it with all your might. Someone said that his father used the lines in the palm of his hand to show the message Mankind Must Work written there. He spoke these words in a forceful tone of voice, tracing the lines with his index finger in the form of an M, another M and finally a W. The son later became a freelancer and worked at home. He said that whenever he had no work and he heard the siren of a police car, he thought in a flash that they were coming to get him. He was burdened with severe feelings of guilt whenever he was not working. Family assignments can be very powerful. Recognizing the messages and testifying to them, talking about them, can help you leave them behind. The healing of your pain points often takes place through knowledge about and insights into your family.

Knowing the Other

People from collective systems are often approached by care workers from the notion of psychological value.[6] In this approach, the failure and the success of the children is related to the parents. In the Netherlands, this notion is often regarded as the one and only truth. With clients from collective systems, nothing might be further from the truth. That is why it's essential to familiarize yourself with your client's background. If you delve into that background, you will know how to formulate your questions. First of all, it is important to know whether someone comes from a collective or from an individual family system. Do children have a psychological or a functional value? Who are the figures of authority, how are decisions made, is it a matriarchal or a patriarchal system and what is the religion? Next, it's important to know someone's migration background and its impact on the family continuity.[7] Once you know where a system goes wrong, you can look for solutions to get that system to work again. If people are vulnerable and anxious because they are going through multiple life phase transitions simultaneously, perhaps they just don't know what to do anymore. Perhaps they've just forgotten that they can call their family. In such cases, as a care worker, you can say something like, my experience is that people from collective systems always help each other in times of need and also find the solutions. So how come that's not happening now? It's often quite easy to go back to where things were working well, and to get the machine working again with a few minor interventions. In other systems, things have been going wrong for three centuries. In such cases, it will not be quite that simple. It is good to know the context you're getting into.

Sacred cows

It is important to be aware of your own sacred cows. Those points of view and ideas that as far as you're concerned can't be called into question, about which there is but one truth. If you're not aware of your own sacred cows, and they're touched on in the dialogue, you'll be very quick to judge. The moment you start to judge, a bell should be ringing right away, wait a minute, I'm now having an opinion about that other person, a sore point from my own cultural baggage has been touched on. For example, one could imagine that arranged marriages for Muslim girls constitute such a sore point for women who fought hard for their liberation. The moment someone else says, I like it that my family chooses a partner for me, as a feminist you'll immediately get furious. Many care workers also have a problem with people who submit to the rules of a religion. Once you know that is my struggle, that is my sore point, you can park it for a while. But if you're not aware of it, you will start judging and feel superior to the other person. This makes safety in the dialogue impossible.

---

6   Kagitçibasi, C. (1996), *Family and Human development across cultures. A view from the other side*. Mahwah, NJ: Lawrence Erlbaum.
7   Tjin A Djie, K. (2003), 'Beschermjassen, een wijze van hulpverlenen waardoor ouders en kinderen uit wijsystemen worden ingebed in hun familie en cultuur', *Systeemtherapie*, 15 (1), pp. 17-39.

Kitlyn:

> *"The fact that parents feel guilty if their children are not doing well was unknown to me from the collective system. As a consequence, I thought it was rubbish, actually. If there was to be an issue of guilt at all, the entire collective system would be to blame for the child not doing well. Stop moaning! If a child wasn't doing well, it should just be taken to task by the system. I just didn't understand. I only knew the one truth, that's what the world is like and that's the way we do it. So, I had to learn to take a good look at my own truth. By studying literature, I came to understand that there is a different way of looking at things in the Western world."*

Switching perspectives

In the intercultural dialogue, it is a condition to be able to switch perspectives. Switching perspectives can only take place in a context that is safe, and free from emotional confusion. That is why it is so important for you to know your own cultural baggage and the cultural baggage of the other person, as well as your sacred cows. If you know that certain beliefs of the other person confuse you, or emotionally upset you, or make you feel unsafe, then you know that you should compose yourself. You will have to apply a bit of force in order to be able to switch to the other person's perspective. If you fail to do that, the essential dialogue will come to a stop. If you very much stick to your own truth, or raise your eyebrows at the other person's beliefs, you will see that the other person will opt out of the conversation. In contacts between care worker and client, it is necessary for both of them to be able to switch to the other's perspective. Both should therefore be able to communicate about their own perspective and that of the other person. A Surinamese client insisted on waiting for his wife, who was still in Suriname, in order to make an important decision about his child. The social worker thought this was ridiculous. Surely the father could act in the interest of his child without the mother? Why wait for the mother? The social worker stopped switching perspectives. If the social worker had been aware of the fact that in her context parents can take over each other's tasks, she could have talked about this and could have asked how this works in her client's system. Then she would have learned that in his system everyone has their own task, which is not so easily taken over by someone else. But when she lets him know three times that she thinks what he wants is crazy, he will feel disqualified. That is emotionally perplexing and puts a stop to switching perspectives. But when it is safe, when you're curious and dare show a personal part of yourself, communication will remain open and you can learn a lot from each other.

Youth protector Chantal explains how she used intercultural competencies with an African family.

"*The mother and the daughter suffer from a post-traumatic war history. The other children don't, as far as is known. The family came into contact with youth protection because the mother had indicated that she wanted to kill herself and take her children with her. I noticed that before it became my case, quite a firm stand had been taken. Afterwards, it became clear that the mother's intention had actually been somewhat different. On that basis, we started working on it. We mainly talked about switching perspectives. In what way does the mother come out with something like that. How is it interpreted here, and what did she actually mean by it? That was our approach. It turned out that using that competency was necessary all the time. Because in this family that pays off tremendously. A concrete example is this mother's use of aggression. In particular the physical aggression in her way of parenting. In Dutch culture, as we see it, this can't be tolerated. That would also have been my approach, I think. Only through giving it more thought, through switching perspectives, we decided to handle this in a different way. And in this way, we managed to put a stop to it. But not by saying that it was just not done, that we wouldn't tolerate it and that's that! More from the perspective of her own way of parenting and at the same time making it clear what is allowed and not allowed here in the Netherlands. We gave her space and opportunities to do things differently, but in her own way. If I hadn't used that competency of switching perspectives, I would very easily have assumed that the norm of whether or not to hit children was as clear to her as it was to me. I think I would have approached her from that angle. Like, you just don't do that, it's not an educational tool. And I think if I had done it that way, I would have achieved very little with this mother.*

Case manager Sjoerd talks about the effectiveness of this way of working in the case of a single Surinamese mother, who has problems raising her children.

We made a genogram and switched perspectives between her culture and ours. We asked questions, such as what it had been like in recent years, what she had learned from her upbringing and what part of this she is using now. So, genogram, context and switching perspectives. Making a genogram is enlightening. You make up the entire picture. What does the family look like, who is living in the Netherlands, who is living elsewhere? You also get a picture of the upbringing in that other country. And how this compares to our parenting norms and values. It's actually clear to me now where the differences lie. You extract the best things and can measure those against the Dutch norms. This woman had parenting support before, but that support had not been working from an intercultural perspective. Whereas that is what's involved when dealing with a family like that. Children who grew up in the Netherlands and a mother who was raised in Suriname. And in this particular case by her grandmother, and not by her own mother. That also makes a difference. It is the kind of information we can put to good use in this way of working. By employing this working method, you can better tailor the care to the insights of the mother herself in parenting questions, and to what she is missing. It also serves to give the mother a bit more time. You have got the mother moving by adapting to her and by addressing her about the good things in her way of parenting. The past three or four months have yielded more than all the help she has had before. We have consulted with the previous care workers. What did they do, where did they miss the connection? That was important for us to know. It was a good way to find out. You learn an awful lot from the other culture you have to associate yourself with. And not only point the finger, but also say, boys, they're not stupid there, they can bring up children too! If I hadn't used the intercultural competencies, it would have been a difficult case. You'll look for where things go wrong, but you won't find out. Now, you're more aware of the fact that these people come from a different culture with different parenting values. From that angle, you learn how to do your job. If you hadn't had that knowledge, you would have just started asking questions as usual. You would have said, all right, this is the problem, now we're going to deploy healthcare without adjusting to that culture. I think we would have come across the same problems again. Saying yes, and then not doing it. But now we have an extremely motivated mother who's working on it. During the first three months she has already tried to do so much, that you almost feel like saying, don't go too fast. Because we still have some way to go, until she herself realizes that she is the power. "

Hidden dimensions

Hidden dimensions are the blind spots in communication. By not being aware of differences in cultures, views and perspectives, for example between the care worker and the client, blind spots in communication are created. These blind spots in turn put a stop to switching perspectives. Previous steps, such as knowing your own baggage, knowledge about the other person and being aware of your sacred cows, your stress points, can clear up many of these blind spots. On the other hand, you should also accept that there will always be hidden dimensions that are not cleared up.

Case manager Bart talks about his blind spot in the contact with a Moroccan family.

"*I have a Moroccan client, a boy from a Moroccan family. The boy was being held at the police station and could not go home. His parents are divorced. The children live with the mother and the father lives elsewhere. The father indicated that he could not always be present at the interviews. This had to do with his health. He was psychologically unstable. Nevertheless, he was always present at the interviews and did most of the talking. The woman with whom the children were living kept a low profile and didn't say much. That in itself provided food for thought. What was happening? On the one hand he says no, but on the other hand he's always there. I had understood from intercultural project member Jeanne that in spite of his divorce he feels responsible as an educator, and that is also part of that culture. This concerned his eldest son. For the second interview I took Jeanne along, and the mother suddenly started playing a more prominent part. Yes, well, I'm a man and that could play a part. Jeanne is a woman, a woman of color too, so this made things a lot simpler. The family aspect also suddenly became much clearer. To the man, his mother was apparently very important and she demanded that he do his best for his son. That's a lot of that kind of information all at once. In one way or another you know about this, also through the training, but to reflect on it in practice and to make use of it is a different matter. Jeanne's support helps me with this. Already during the first interview with the parents it kept being said that the boy would be better off with family living in Amsterdam. A sister of the father lives there, with her husband and two children. That family is doing well, they run a kebab place. The children go to school, the boy was welcome there. But I didn't hear that, didn't latch on to it. I wasn't even thinking about it. I already had another plan up my sleeve. A program involving a short period of detention in a juvenile detention center, followed by intensive ambulatory guidance. I had already signed him up for that. So the Amsterdam story did not come in at all handy for me. Anyway, when I got Jeanne involved, she pointed this out to me. Saying like, how does it work? How about the Amsterdam story? Are you the one to decide whether or not that's allowed? It got quiet for a while then. I had to think. I did a lot of ignoring, I suppose. When Jeanne came along on a house call, the Amsterdam story was given plenty of space. That brought about a major change. Those people felt heard. Their entire family was more or less discussed now. With that, a piece of history also became clear. At a certain point the cultural differences were mentioned. The importance of family for them, and how different things are in the Netherlands. In that way, it became a different interview. Amsterdam became a serious possibility. So that's what we're going to do. Meanwhile, I have been in contact with the sister in Amsterdam. That, too, was a revelation. She had lots of things to say about this boy and about her brother. How much she worries, how involved she is and what she could do for him.*"

Communicating with compassion and empathy

The philosopher Roman Krznaric wrote the book *Empathy, introspection is out, outrospection is in!* (2015). He developed a fascination with the theme because he discovered that he had lost his feelings of empathy after a traumatic event. His mother died when he was eight.

Krznaric in an interview:

" I was in my study at Oxford. I was thinking about what her death had meant for my life. I knew that I, like many children who have experienced something traumatic, suddenly no longer remembered anything about the time before. But I had also lost my feelings of empathy. The ability to empathize with others, their joys, their sorrows. After her death I rarely ever laughed or cried. What I realized then, what was revealed to me, was that my interest in empathy stemmed from an unconscious desire to regain my lost empathetic self. "[8]

---

8   Krznaric, R. (2015), *Empathy*. Rider.

We can recognize this in clients, but also in colleagues and in ourselves. Somewhere within us or in the Other there is often a story, a great loss, a traumatic event. And if the environment is not available, for example because the father himself mourns the death of his wife and the grandparents the loss of their daughter, the trauma cannot be dealt with. So you're no longer able to understand, to switch perspectives and to empathize.

Arnold, a student, said that he was nine years old when his mother found a new partner. Until then, he had always been her help and stay. But from then on he became withdrawn. He hated that man. However, there was one teacher at school who noticed that something was wrong. She had asked him to tell her about it, and he had felt supported then. Now that he told the story at Kitlyn's training session and relived it in the safe group, he was able to look at his own story with compassion and empathy. If you can do that towards yourself, you can also do it towards the Other.

We need feelings of empathy in order to learn how to live, to know who we are and to relate to the Other. According to biologist De Waal, humans as well as animals are born with this ability, but we turn our backs on it partly due to the ideas of the theory of evolution: Man is said to be selfish by nature.[9] De Waal contradicts this, and one of the studies he cites to this end shows that toddlers get more satisfaction from treating others than from getting a treat themselves.[10]

Child psychiatrist Bruce Perry is of the same opinion. From studies cited in his book *Born for love* (2010) it would seem that having strong relationships with others is a prerequisite for happiness, health and a long life. It reduces the risks of depression and anxiety disorders. In fact, altruism makes you happier than selfishness, and that's not just the case for adults. However, Perry says, we are no longer equipped to learn to switch perspectives:

> *During most of the past 150.000 years people have been living in groups, together with multiple generations and multiple families. These relatively small tribes were characterized by rich human interactions, which is not often the case in Western societies. (...) Children were surrounded by fathers, sisters, uncles, older cousins, nieces, nephews, aunts and other relatives, all of them individuals who could teach them something, take them to task, nurture them and enrich them.*[11]

According to the aforementioned scientists, the seeds of empathy are there. However, feelings of empathy are often stifled by personal traumas and social attitudes to individuality and autonomy.

It is beyond doubt that every client likes to deal with an empathetic care worker who has compassion. Empathy means being able to walk in someone else's shoes, which goes beyond sympathy. It's putting yourself in the other person's place.

Compassion means that you are there, present, you're completely at the other

---

9   Waal, F. de (2009), *Een tijd voor empathie*. Contact.
10 Waal, F. de (2013), *De Bonobo en de tien geboden*. Atlas Contact.
11 Perry, B. and M. Szalavitz (2011), *Born for love*. HarperCollins Publishers Inc.

person's disposal. The Tibetan Buddhist Lama Michel Rinpoche once gave a lecture on compassion in mental healthcare. He said the following: 'The meaning of compassion in Tibetan is that we have a strong desire for others to be free from suffering. Sometimes we think that having compassion means that we are very much emotionally involved with others, but it's not like that. Compassion doesn't mean that we suffer from the suffering of others.'

You can bring empathy and compassion back into your life and your work, you can learn it and practice it if you have lost it. Krznaric, De Waal and Perry all argue for this. You can start by paying attention to the way in which you communicate. As the Tibetan Lama Healer Lama Gangchen Rinpoche wrote in the foreword to our book *De Familieziel (The Family Soul)* (2013):

> *(...) It is essential that we use our five senses in a positive way in all interactions, starting with the day-to-day relationships with our partner and children. Once we are able to turn all our contacts with our family at home into positive ones, we will automatically create a peaceful atmosphere in our home. From there, we can continue to create positive relationships in society. We can begin by simply observing our manner of speaking, listening, looking, touching, et cetera in our everyday life. Are we aggressive or gentle? Is our tone of voice loud or friendly? And what are the results? It's very simple: if we speak harshly, the other person will be insulted and angry, and we probably won't get what we want. Whereas if we speak in a friendly tone of voice, the other person will feel pleased and be happy to be of help to us.* [12]

If you, as a care worker, are empathetic yourself and full of compassion towards others, then you are a protective wrap and others will be able to open themselves up to you. Then healing can take place. As becomes clear in the case of Sven, described in detail by Irene in book form[13]:

Sven is an adolescent with a mild intellectual disability, and diagnosed with ODD (oppositional-defiant disorder). Due to his behavioral problems, he hasn't been living at home from the age of twelve; his mother cannot take care of him and his father has only recently come into the picture again. At the age of seventeen, after wanderings around youth care land, he ends up in a Very Intensive Treatment group at the Ambiq remedial educational center. At the age of seventeen Sven develops leukemia, and Ambiq makes the unorthodox decision to continue taking care of him until the end. A temporary treatment setting is not suited to his new situation, but he feels at home there and yet another move in this vulnerable phase would be too much for him. The team does everything in its power to do what is necessary and they put their hearts and souls into making possible what in normal circumstances would not be possible. All his wishes to be close to the people he loves – family as well as professionals – are granted.

---

12 Tjin A Djie, K. en I. Zwaan (2013), *De Familieziel, hoe je geschiedenis je kan helpen op je levenspad*. Amsterdam: Prometheus Bert Bakker.
13 Zwaan, I. (2016), *Sven tot het einde, de complexe praktijk rondom een puber met een LVB, ODD en een levensbedreigende ziekte*. Assen: Koninklijke van Gorcum.

Because of the protective wraps with which Sven is surrounded after the leukemia diagnosis, during the disease process and in the last phase of his life, his behavioral disorder vanishes completely, and he lives months longer than the doctors had predicted.

Finally

There are different methods and strategies available to put your own story and that of your client forward. The use of genograms, contextual questions, the lifeline, the TOPOI model and testimonials are useful tools to deploy in the intercultural dialogue. These tools are extensively discussed in chapter 7.

Assignment

- To what extent do you know your own cultural and historical baggage?
- What are your sacred cows?
- What kind of beliefs or behavior of other people make your hair stand on end?
- Can you give an example of when that happened in relation to a client, colleague or co-student?
- Can you imagine how you could act in a case like that, with the knowledge you have now acquired?
- How can you create safety for all those involved in an incident of conflicting views and values? Please give an example from practice.

7

Instruments for the intercultural dialogue

Kitlyn: "Western psychology is very much I-centered. It is mainly about feelings and emotions. Questions like 'what do you feel', 'what do you want yourself' and similar phraseology just don't work for people from collective systems. Because they are socialized in the relationship with the group, and not as an autonomous individual. It really drives them mad when people keep asking them those kinds of questions."

The greatest success factor in the dialogue with the Other is the relationship between the person requiring care and the care worker.[1] There is a good chance for the care contact to succeed once the relationship has taken proper shape. A number of factors can be distinguished in this process.[2] First of all, it has proven to be very important to connect with the client's strengths and perspectives. The focus should not be on the method of care, but on the possibilities and wishes the client can relate to. Secondly, it is evident that if the client experiences the relationship with the care worker as positive and supportive, this will benefit its development. The relationship is particularly felt to be positive when a warm contact has been established, whereby the client feels accepted and heard. Furthermore, it has become apparent that in order to increase the chances of success, the client must have faith in the approach chosen. Finally, it is important that the care organization applies procedures that support the aforementioned basic assumptions.

This chapter discusses a number of instruments that can be deployed either individually or in combination in the contact between client and care worker. These instruments are aimed at examining your own cultural baggage and sacred cows, those of your client, and the relationship between the two. The instruments contribute to a better understanding of each other, so that the relationship will acquire its proper shape and the chosen care approach responds as closely as possible to the client's needs. First of all, the genogram is discussed, a method which serves to illustrate an entire family system, with its strengths and weaknesses. Next, contextual questions are dealt with. If you cannot ask about emotions and feelings of the client from a collective system, how do you formulate your questions? Following this, we briefly describe the lifeline, after which we go through the TOPOI model, an analysis model for the intercultural dialogue, aimed at examining the relationship between client and care worker. Then, we pay attention to the positive role played by life stories. Finally, the testimony is explained as an instrument for healing. For each instrument, it is explained how it combines with previous instruments.

Genograms[3]

A genogram is a visual overview of a person's family ties, made up of a number of standard symbols. It schematically shows a family structure over multiple generations. In addition to the actual family tree data, the genogram can provide information about life phase transitions such as migration, birth, death, illness and divorce. It can also reveal information about interaction patterns, figures of authority, black sheep, dominant attitudes, strategies for maintaining the dialogue

---

1 Clark, M.D. (2001), 'Change-focussed Youth Work', *Journal of the Center for Families, Children and the Courts*.
2 Hout, A. van en K. Tjin A Djie (2007), 'Van hulpverlening naar zelfredzaamheid'. In: S. Spinder, L. Joanknecht, A. van Hout en R. van Pagée (eds.), *Krachten en Kansen, Initiatieven voor vernieuwing in zorg en welzijn*. Bohn Stafleu van Loghum.
3 Parts of this paragraph and the models were inspired by: Jessurun, C.M. (1994), 'Genogrammen en etniciteit'. In: J. Hoogsteder (ed.), *Etnocentrisme en communicatie in de hulpverlening, module 4: interculturele hulpverlening*. Utrecht St. Landelijke Federatie Welzijnsorganisaties voor Surinamers, pp. 171-194.

in the family, how a family makes decisions, and so on. Figure 7.1 provides an overview of the major symbols in a genogram.

Symbols

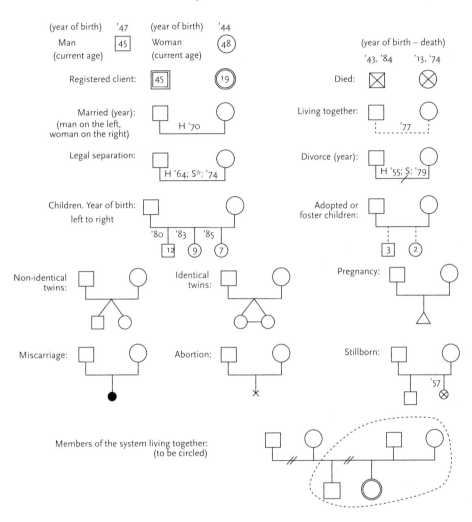

Figure 7.1 The major symbols in a genogram

The children's row is listed in order of age. In the squares and circles, the year of birth of the person concerned is indicated, with next to it the year of death, if applicable. If a person has migrated, this is indicated with an m + year. Under the two branches there is room for specific information and remarks about the branch in question. If you would like to indicate other items in the drawing, create a symbol or marking yourself. For example, give a color to the figures of authority in the system. A basic genogram looks like figure 7.2.

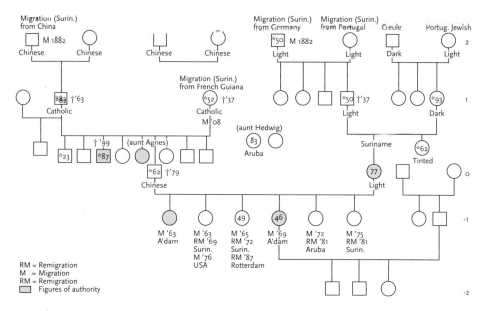

Figure 7.2 Basic genogram

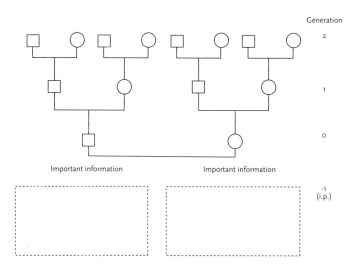

Figure 7.3 Genogram of Kitlyn Tin A Djie

Figure 7.3 shows Kitlyn's genogram.[4] In this genogram five generations are depicted. Migration and remigration data are included, which provides insight in how the family is spread across the world. Next, the figures of authority are marked. This, in combination with the migration data, assumes a complex consultation structure. The lines connect the figures of authority. For the first generation skin

---

4 This genogram was published previously in: Tjin A Djie, K. (2000), 'Ouderschap in een wij-systeem', Second Alice van der Pas Lecture.

color is also indicated. Skin color says a lot about attitudes and positions. This genogram was made in response to problems concerning the grandson of one of Kitlyn's sisters. It was not possible for him to live with his mother. The entire family participated in solving the problem. Figures of authority consulted with those involved in order to create support for a decision. They found a solution, which was that the child went to live with his grandfather, with everyone's consent. If this four-year-old boy had been in the Netherlands and had come into contact with Bureau Jeugdzorg here, what would have happened? In all probability the family guardian would have found all this interference bad for the child, and the child would have been placed in care.

Genograms are often seen as a set of squares and circles that together form a family tree. But a genogram is actually a very powerful instrument to uncover life stories. Not only the factual story with dates and events is told, but also how it is perceived. When people are invited to tell their life story by means of a genogram, they are forced to provide a form of continuity and overview. At times of chaos in their lives, people often like to have an overview, to be reminded of where they stand in the general scheme and of all those standing around them. In the confusion surrounding the problems, parents have often forgotten who their sources of strength are. Sometimes people say that they have no one at all anymore. But through a genogram they nevertheless discover a figure of support whom they can call upon. It restores relationships. Telling the story in itself is often healing. It is important that a genogram is always queried about a specific theme. The theme chosen, which can for example be inferred from the care requested, can be used as a common thread in the interview. A theme can be disease, death, the supernatural, religion, disqualification, you name it. When you ask who are the ones linked to that theme, people will come into the picture whom the client did not previously have in mind. The story is suddenly seen in a different light. Like oh, that's why I had poor contact with that grandmother. Or, hey, I can go and talk to that aunt. Forgotten opportunities and possibilities may manifest themselves. A genogram brings back forgotten memories. It works like a protective wrap.

Case manager Henke explains to what extent the genogram has helped her to gain insight into the problems of a family, and the required direction the care should take. It concerns a Dutch father and a Croatian mother. The children are abused and neglected by the mother. The father is at work during the day. Both parents turn out to carry many secrets about their past within them.

> *"Twice I used a genogram with this family. Initially during the second or third interview, as an introduction, to gain a little more insight. The second time I used it to find out with them what the possibilities were for a family network consultation. The second time in particular it triggered much discussion. That paper was a really good basis for getting people to talk about heavy topics. It was also a way to give each other space. Because sometimes it was about her family, and other times about his family. Because it was all being drawn, people came into the picture, which set stories in motion. In the end it made the system much clearer. We looked for people who would*

qualify for the family consultation. What was special, was that when making the genogram, it transpired that the father had been partly raised in a different family. A family with 13 children, and a number of those people are still of great importance to him. I really wondered if we would have discussed these figures of support at all if we hadn't used the model.

I used the genogram that I had drawn on a flip chart the first time as a starting point for the second interview. I noticed that emotionally charged subjects were easier to discuss via the paper, because they were focused on the flip chart. There were a large number of people in it whom they had lost over time. Especially in those cases the paper seemed to reconnect them with those people. For me, too, it is a pleasant model. It was not so much that they were telling me something, but rather that they referred to times past amongst themselves. I thought that was beautiful.

It has provided me with a much broader picture of the system that envelops these people. Whereas I initially thought it was a small system, it turned out to be quite a large one, with a number of figures of support. As it happened, there were plenty of opportunities for setting up the family consultation. It also strengthened the relationship between us, because via the genogram they told me a lot of things, and in return received my respect for their stories. And I empathized with their situation. Whereas previously they had tended to feel caught out by the care worker, it seems like we have now taken a step towards collaboration. To change the situation and to make them aware of the fact that that is a good thing for the children. Not so much that we have come up with that, but rather that they themselves have realized that the current situation is not good for the children.

What emerged during intervision when looking at this genogram, is that this family has suffered many losses. This mother has already lost two children. The father has lost important figures of support in his life. By using this model, by looking at it in this way, a different approach has been taken. We have said that we will try to prevent further experiences of loss. We will focus on not having to take those children away from home. We met with the care workers involved with the mother. They indicated that because of all that trauma, the mother had never actually been properly socialized in the Netherlands. We would not have arrived at that conclusion otherwise. Resocializing can be a starting point for change. This means that these people will very practically have to start looking for a place to live, and what neighborhood will be preferable for that. They have responded very well to this. It is special to see that you're actually taking an entirely different turn. I have also noticed that when you're so close to such a family, they are much more alert as to their own actions. It gives the mother space to breathe that she can think, you're not here to take my children away from me. That is of course often a great fear. But you're here to see who I can be, that I'm allowed to be here. That really does give her space. "

A genogram is a good way for care workers to uncover their own cultural baggage and sacred cows, to enable them to use their own story in order to invite the client to tell his story. And to maintain the dialogue with that other person. After all, once you're aware of your own set ideas, you can park them for a while in order to remain in the other person's context. During intervision sessions or work consultations, care workers can question each other about their own genograms. You can then go in search of important life phase transitions, dominant attitudes, black sheep and strategies to keep the dialogue going. By making a genogram together with your client, you're more or less forced to remain in the other person's context. That helps to switch perspectives and gain more understanding. It also helps to build up a relationship. It can be a ritual activity that provides distraction and creates an atmosphere of conviviality and trust. A genogram consists of at least three generations. That, too, is essential to remain with the other person and stop reasoning on the basis of your own frame of reference. An important function of making genograms with your client is to reveal blind spots about strengths in families. When children have to be taken into care, many care workers forget to consider family members who might be able to offer a (temporary) home. After all, it is much better to accommodate children in their own nest rather than with an unknown foster family. Genograms always involve asking contextual questions, as discussed in the next paragraph.

Contextual questions

When the client's genogram has been drawn, together with the care worker, the client is interviewed about the story behind the drawing. Instead of asking I-focused questions, such as "how do you feel" and "what would you like yourself", the genogram invites you to ask context-related questions. That means questions about the system. In doing this, it is important that you as a care worker don't dominate, but that you position yourself on the sidelines, listening. Let the parents know that together with them you intend to go and look for the sources of strength in their system. You, as a care worker, would like their advice on possible solutions. You help the family to regain control of their lives. The following questions are important.

- Who have migrated? (visualize in genogram)
- What are your ways, traditions, values, norms?
- Are men or women the boss in your family?
- Who are the figures of authority, who take important decisions? (visualize in genogram)
- How do these decisions come about, how does that work?
- What effect has migration had on decision making?
- (In what way) is there still contact with the figures of authority?
- Who are the figures of support, who helps you, or used to help you before the migration, in times of trouble? (visualize in genogram)
- What are the pros and cons of the culture of origin? What would you like to hold on to and what would you like to abandon?
- What are the pros and cons of living in the Netherlands? Where does it clash? What is going well?
- How would the problem be solved in the country of origin?

When figures of authority come into the picture, it is important to involve them in looking for solutions. Figures of authority in the family often don't reside in the Netherlands. In those cases, it is good to advise the family to consult them by Skype, telephone or email. The parent or the child can also be asked to put themselves in the place of the figure of authority. This is likewise a possibility if the figure of authority in question has died. If the grandmother is the figure of authority, you ask the client: "What would grandma advise you to do now? What would grandma advise the care workers? Who would help grandma to make or implement this decision?" In case of a custodial placement you do not initially ask a child: "Where would you like to live?", but you ask those involved: "Where would grandma like the child to live in the family?" Such questions are of course also important if no genogram has been made.

The lifeline

In chapter 5 we saw how life phase transitions take place from separation via the liminal phase up to incorporation. We also described that migrants with traumas often find themselves in the liminal phase and that old, unresolved trauma frequently surfaces when new difficult events in life occur. A distinction can be made between normal life phase transitions, such as the transition from child to puberty, adolescence, having a child or getting older. In addition, there are the special life phase transitions, the more radical events that have a major influence, such as premature death, chronic illness and involuntary unemployment. Migration and flight are special life phase transitions. The vulnerability increases when the special life phase transition occurs during a normal life phase transition.

When together with your client you draw a lifeline, which contains all the important events, the life phase transitions, you will gain insight into the history of your client and you will be able to recognize the layers in the experiences of loss.[5] It is often important to place several generations side by side; that way, you discover patterns that are passed on from generation to generation. Or you discover what happened in the lives of parents and grandparents that caused them to be unavailable, for example.

How do you draw a lifeline? You always start with the client's own lifeline, before placing two previous generations next to it. With a ruler you draw a vertical line on a sheet of paper. To the left of the line, you write the dates and years of events, and to the right of the line the event and the age at which a life phase transition occurred. You start at the top, to the left of the line, with the date of birth. Major life phase transitions include relocations, migration, flight, changes of school or job, marriages, divorces, travel, accidents and illness, the death of loved ones, births to close family, wars, disasters, violence, graduation, and so on. Fill it in as completely as possible.

---

5   Rhmaty, F. (2011), *Traumaverwerking met vluchtelingen*. Assen: Koninklijke Van Gorcum.

So, in the first instance, you visualize as many important events as possible. At the same time, you can gradually discern a cohesion. If, for example, there has been a relocation, followed shortly thereafter by the death of a grandparent and a divorce of the parents, you can reflect on the enormous impact that phase must have on the life of your client and that of his family. Perhaps it has led to anxiety, depression, and the problems at hand. That way you can trace the origin of current themes.

Events often remain unresolved if there was no safety net at the time. After all, when something bad happens, the whole family might be upset, so that they cannot take care of each other. For example, at the time of their divorce, the migration, the death of a child, the parents were too preoccupied with themselves and, therefore, were not available for their children. That is why it is important to know the context around events. Who were involved, how long did it take, was there support from the family for the parents, for the child? These and other contextual questions you can ask while trying to interpret events.[6]

TOPOI[7]

P. Watzlawick[8] developed five axioms[9] for communication:
1. One cannot not communicate.
2. Every form of communication has a content aspect and a relational aspect.
3. The nature of a relationship depends on the punctuation of the course of events.
4. Communication proceeds in a digital as well as an analog way.
5. Every form of communication is either symmetrical (equal) or complementary (additional).

Based on Watzlawick's five axioms, the Interaction Academy in Antwerp developed the TOPOI model. In Greek, *Topoi* means 'places', think, for example, of the word 'topography'. The TOPOI model helps to map, evaluate and research the intercultural communication. Edwin Hoffman refined and developed the TOPOI model into an analysis and intervention framework. Each of the letters in Dutch represents an aspect of communication. For each aspect there is an appropriate key question.[10]

---

6 Tjin A Djie, K. en I. Zwaan (2013), *De Familieziel, hoe je geschiedenis je kan helpen op je levenspad*. Amsterdam: Prometheus Bert Bakker.
7 Parts of this paragraph are based on Hoffman, E. en F. Ogunc-Serap (1996), 'Interculturele gespreksvoering'. In: J. de Jong en M. van den Berg (eds.), *Transculturele Psychiatrie & Psychotherapie, handboek voor hulpverlening en beleid*. Swets & Zeitling publishers.
8 Watzlawick, W., J.H. Beavin en D.D. Jackson (2014). *Pragmatics of Human Communication*. W.W. Norton & Company Ltd.
9 An axiom is a statement regarded as established, without having been proven.
10 Hoffman, E. (2002), *Interculturele gespreksvoering. Theorie en praktijk van het TOPOI-model*. Houten: Bohn Stafleu van Loghum.

T	=	Taal (Language)	Do we understand each other's language?
O	=	Ordening (Arrangement)	Is our communication based on the same frame of reference?
P	=	Perspectief (Perspective)	Which personal perspectives play a role?
O	=	Organisatie (Organization)	Does someone know how things are organized?
I	=	Inzet (Effort)	Do we make enough effort to understand each other?

TOPOI is an important checklist for identifying misunderstandings in intercultural communication. It is based on systems thinking, from the assumption that people interact with each other. That is why it is very much in line with 'Protective wraps'. Edwin Hoffman always starts his workshops by explaining that not cultures, but people talk to each other. Many misunderstandings arise because people don't understand each other, or because they remain stuck in their own truth. TOPOI is always about interaction. In practice it is impossible to distinguish the different aspects of communication. But as a useful instrument for analysis, we go through them one by one, in order to detect hiccups and bottlenecks in communication.

Language

Earlier in this book, we discussed the importance of language in relation to identity. How difficult it is to express your emotions, or to be able to say exactly what you mean, in a language that is not your own. For a care worker, it is important to give some thought to this. What is considered humorous? And how is this responded to? This is different everywhere. Or the way sadness is expressed. Another important part of language is its nonverbal symbolism, which differs from culture to culture. Nodding yes and shaking no, raising your thumb, pointing at your forehead, every culture has its own nonverbal signals. Waving your hand along your ear, for example, while saying 'mmm' because you really like something you're eating or drinking, is typically Dutch and even just across the border it is no longer recognized. Then there is the language of unwritten rules for how to treat each other. The way of greeting. Do you shake hands or not? Do you make much or little eye-to-eye contact? Where do you sit down? How do you use your voice? All those things are important to consider. It is essential to examine how the other person's habits relate to yours. Perhaps it will touch upon your sacred cows. As a female care worker, you might find it difficult if a Moroccan man is not used to shaking hands with you. But to park that sacred cow for a while can contribute to creating a safe environment, which is a prerequisite for an open dialogue. In chapter 4, attention was paid to the indirect style of communicating in collective systems, which frequently makes Western care workers cringe. Because people from collective systems are less direct and sometimes communicate in a roundabout way, Dutch care workers get confused and they don't think it's fair that, in their eyes, the client doesn't speak the truth. We also saw that second-generation migrants in particular are constantly commuting between cultures and loyalties, which makes them say different things in different contexts. This, too, is an aspect of language that you should be aware of. It goes without saying that if the client and the care worker don't understand each other because the client has insufficient command of Dutch, an interpreter should be engaged.

Arrangement

This aspect is about the way in which everyone arranges their own reality. Because everyone has a different frame of reference, looks at the world from different angles. It is a given that from one person to the next, the world is arranged differently. Once you can see through this, you can accept it and it will not hinder communication. An example of different ways of arranging things is the individual system and the collective system. And the consequence that Western care is aimed at the individual, while the client from the collective system puts the interests of the group first.

Perspectives

To be able to switch perspectives, you must be able to put yourself in the other person's perspective. This means you have to be acquainted with that perspective. TOPOI talks about two types of perspectives that can be distinguished in communication: the interpersonal perspective and the social perspective. The interpersonal perspective is about the substantive and the relational message that people convey to each other in communication. They don't just want to convey a substantive message, they also want the other person to respond to it in a certain way. And vice versa. For example, as a male Dutch care worker you might expect a Moroccan woman to also give her opinion, whereas only her husband is speaking. This might require a different kind of effort than just addressing the woman about her contribution to the conversation.

The social perspective is about the attitudes and messages that exist in society. The dominant discourse in society, for example that everyone should be able to speak Dutch properly, can lead to a certain perspective for the care worker, who might be annoyed that the client doesn't speak Dutch, when he's been living in the Netherlands for 40 years.

Organization

The policy of the care organization can have a major influence on the communication between care worker and client. If clients have to sign the treatment plan, this frequently causes instant hiccups in communication. People are often not prepared to ritually confirm their own problems with a signature. Or they may not be able to write, which gives rise to a block. Or clients bring a present, which the care worker is not allowed to accept. That also stands in the way of good contact. Other problems are bureaucracy, the lack of clarity about "where should I go" in the maze of healthcare institutions in the Netherlands. The limited number of interviews allowed within that institution, the trust that cannot be built up as a consequence, and so on.

Effort

It is important that in the interviews both parties show commitment to make an effort. If an effort is made, appreciation and trust will be given. In that case there is a willingness to work on the smooth running of the care process. Sometimes it is difficult for a care worker to make an effort, when serious facts such as abuse and neglect are involved. That is where the sacred cows pop up again. Nevertheless, it is important to know what the effect is of your efforts. If you take a judgmental position, you close the gates and tension will arise in the client. Observing the client's behavior and communicating about it can help to open the gates again. It will give the client room for expressing emotions. This will inspire trust in the client, as a result of which he will sooner be prepared to make an effort.

Combining TOPOI with genograms

If a care worker brings in a case in intervision or supervision, you can almost always be certain that the theme encountered by the care worker also appears in his own genogram. Because there's a sensitive point there, a sacred cow. Or it can also be a big blind spot, it's not noticed. The answers to questions about cases asked by care workers are to be found in their own genogram. What is enlightening, is to compare the genogram of the client with that of the care worker. It is important to formulate a clear question about the case. Next, you put TOPOI between the two genograms and you investigate where the malfunction is. Frequently the care worker soon sees what it's about.

Case manager Marthin:

> " *I am the youngest in a Moluccan family. I know about myself that I very much have a wait-and-see attitude. You just happen to be the youngest. And whenever you said something you were looked at like, you think you have something to add? You're not taken very seriously, because your older brothers or sisters always know better. So, your position within your family is actually quite decisive. During the training I made that link. Where you come from partly determines your position in groups. Subjects that come up in certain families and that are also important to you are highlighted by you. Unconsciously.* "

Life story

Genograms and lifelines provide the contours to unlock a life story. By telling life stories, you see people who have become unbalanced be revitalized. The story often works as a kind of protective wrap. In your story lies your identity. That is why it's good to know your story, and to tell it, particularly during a difficult period. When you have lost your identity for a while. Life stories help to provide continuity. To keep the stories of children in foster care complete, they have their own life book with them. This book with photographs, stories and drawings goes along to every context they end up in. It shapes continuity in their life.

Professor of social sciences Christien Brinkgreve describes how her desire for knowledge, for understanding, for looking for broader connections, for knowing the stories behind stories, was partly shaped in her youth.

> "My mother suffered from severe depressions that kept recurring, and had something scary, and also mysterious, for us as children. We always saw it coming, you saw it in her eyes, you heard it in her voice. It was a different world she ended up in, a terrifying world that she feared, time and time again, she would never get out of anymore. It was like a natural catastrophe: it set in, it could not be driven away, it controlled everything. And at a certain point it was all over.
> We went through it and didn't understand it. I wanted to know what happened then, what made her collapse like she fell into a hellish pit and the exit was blocked. And why we couldn't help her. And also: how I could prevent myself from also falling into that pit later on. If I understood what caused it, perhaps I would be able to avoid or prevent such fearful tumbles."

She examines the power of stories as regards knowing, creating order, creating a new order.

Most cultures have great storytelling traditions. Fairytales, myths, tales and anecdotes about ancestors meet the need for orientation and meaning. Who are we and how do we treat each other? What is good and what is evil? What do we find important and what should we do in life? Stories help you experience being part of a larger whole, and what place you occupy in the community.[11]

In the west we have somewhat lost this tradition, and we usually no longer try to find out who we are in relation to the environment, family, history and culture that we carry within us. We try to look within to get to know ourselves. However, for the identity building of children it is extremely important to know where you come from, who belong with you and what the history of your family is. For example, about two thirds of all the children in Amsterdam have two or more ethnicities. They frequently know nothing about this, neither are they usually stimulated to find out about it. But it is important to connect with your contexts. Paying attention to this is possible through the story. Because stories are like a protective wrap; they help you to become embedded in your safe environment.

Memories and life stories allow us to experience continuity and coherence in our life, to connect with our social environment and to maintain our self-esteem and self-confidence, especially when living conditions test us.[12] Gibson: "People who are approaching death often tend to extensively look back on their lives. On many occasions, this functions as a reconciliation with life. At a younger age, people

---

11 Brinkgreve, C. (2014), *Vertel, over de kracht van verhalen*. Atlas Contact.
12 Bohlmeijer, E. (2007), 'Herinneringen, levensverhalen en gezondheid'. In: E. Bohlmeijer, L. Mies en G. Westerhof, *De betekenis van levensverhalen, theoretische beschouwingen en toepassingen in onderzoek en praktijk*, pp. 31-39. Houten: Bohn Stafleu van Loghum.

mainly take stock by looking back on their past. At that time the overview may give rise to new choices in life." In case of other major events such as illness, death and violence, people also often feel the need to look back. Bohlmeijer: "The experience is that something that was whole is now broken. And it takes courage and strength to develop and maintain a new identity or a positive self-image." People who find themselves in two or more life phase transitions benefit from telling their life story. It helps to shape transition in the liminal phase between then and now, the transitional space. In that vulnerable period of loss, where nothing new has yet replaced the old, life stories can fulfill an important role as an anchor before moving on to something new. It has all the ingredients of a protective wrap, because everyone and everything from the past plays a part in it. Family, culture, food, living environment, employment record, education, ambitions, in short, too much to mention. When making a genogram and a lifeline, it is important to be aware of the function served by telling the story. That makes it possible for you to optimally facilitate this process with lots of warmth and attention.

Testimony[13]

Testimony therapy gives people with a traumatic experience the opportunity to testify about it. Research among former political prisoners in Chile shows that testifying about their experiences had a positive effect on their stress complaints. By telling the story, experiences gain significance and can be put in a meaningful perspective. Not only serious traumas can be healed through testimony, other bumps from the past, family assignments and unpleasant experiences, can also be given a place by talking about them. By bringing experiences to light, sharing stories you never dared to tell with important people in your environment, people who are linked to the story, healing of old wounds can take place. According to the shamans, by transforming old patterns, seven generations before you and seven generations after you are cured of pain in the family. They could be people from your family you tell the story to, or important friends. But they could also be total strangers. Telling your story often makes things fall into place, allowing them to be accepted for what they are. They have been given a place as a story. This effect can also occur when making a genogram with your client.

Behavioral scientist Gré experienced a moment of healing by telling her story during a training with Kitlyn.

> *"When I was 15, my father died and I left school to help my mother around the house. Later on, I started evening lessons, a secretarial training. I ended up as a secretary at the university in the psychiatry department. There I discovered that I was capable of more than being a secretary. From the reports I had to type I thought: there's such a lot going wrong with young people. I was very much interested in all that. In the end I opted for*

---

[13] Dijk, J. van en B. Schreuder (2001), 'De getuigenis als therapie. Beschrijving van een kortdurende therapeutische methode voor getraumatiseerde slachtoffers van politiek geweld', *Tijdschrift voor Psychotherapie*, 27.

orthopedagogics. At first I hardly knew what it was, but I gradually found out. When I was 26, I started working part-time and studying. Then I graduated. At first, I only had jobs that had nothing to do with care. At some stage I went to a career counseling agency to find out what I was able to do and what I wanted to do. There I met someone from my time in psychiatry, a child psychologist. He said, why don't you start doing something with your studies. Why do you start new studies? Because that's what I kept doing, all kinds of studies and courses. I always felt, there's things I can do, but I don't know exactly what. At one point I got the feeling, which I found difficult, that on the one hand I was transcending my milieu and on the other hand I didn't yet belong anywhere. I was in a kind of limbo. During my studies I wrote a thesis on young Turks and Moroccans. I read a lot of books on living between two cultures. And as a matter of fact, I recognized myself in that. I no longer belonged anywhere. As if there are secret codes of conduct through which others immediately recognized that I didn't belong in that student world.

I started puzzling a bit about what happened during that training with Kitlyn. It was about where you come from. Specifics, characteristics, what is your own, what isn't. I had been kind of looking for that. What about me, where do I belong? What feels like my roots? I think I've always been free from judging others. Kitlyn begged to differ. That's not possible, you must have something, something specific! She made a remark that rather intrigued me. I had something like what do you mean, different cultures. That people are specific in their own right, go looking for their roots, the house where they were born, try and find out things. I had doubts about that in my case. I didn't have that primal feeling of that's where I belong. And then at some point something happened to me. Like, oh yeah, wait a minute.

During adolescence I went through a period when I had no appreciation for my father's position at all. He was a sail maker and could have become head of his department, but he didn't want that. He deliberately just wanted to stay with his colleagues in the group. He didn't want to be above them. I said, what nonsense! Come on! You must do it! I couldn't understand it. I wanted to be able to say that my father was head of the department. Later I started to really appreciate his decision. I actually admired him for making this choice. I am who I am, I am happy in this job. Whereas I myself really wanted to get somewhere.

I was born in the Tuinbouwstraat in Groningen. My parents are both from the Oosterparkwijk, a disadvantaged area. One of them comes from the red village, the other from the blue village. When I was a child we often went there, because my grandmother and other members of the family still lived there. One way or another I apparently identified with that, even though I never lived there myself. At present, the Oosterparkwijk evokes pride, unlike it did in the past. In the old days, when someone said something about the Oosterparkwijk, I thought, I'd better not say that my parents come from there. And now I no longer have that at all. The people there were simple, but they stood by what they said. That's what's happened during the training. That I thought, if there is something I can call my own, then that's what comes to mind. It makes me move more freely. You sometimes have a part within you that you hide, that you deny, that you don't show. It is much easier now to say, that's me as well. In general, I'm quite calm. But in an argument, I can suddenly get fierce. And also a bit unreasonable. Then I think, yes, that's me as well. And I say, oh yeah, that's my *background. At such times my voice suddenly gets much louder. The healing is in the fact that it's simply allowed to be there.* "

Finally

From here we go to the final chapter. Chapter 8 discusses the implications for the care sector in more detail. What does 'Protective wraps' mean for care workers, and how does it relate to the methodologies currently in force? In what way can you incorporate 'Protective wraps' in your work?

Assignment

- Make a lifeline of yourself in relation to two generations before you (for example your mother and your grandmother, or your father and your grandfather).
- Draw a genogram over at least three generations, based on a theme that plays a role in your family.
- Make a lifeline and a genogram with a client, or a co-student.
- Describe your experiences and results.

8

New perspective in care

Kitlyn: "The Netherlands has a history of colonialism and slavery. Many migrants require care. They come from countries where the entire tribal network has remained behind. In Amsterdam, some 180 nationalities live together. 64% of children up to 14 years of age have a migration background there.[1] So it can just make me feel angry that no thought is being given on how care methodologies can be adapted to Dutch multicultural society."

---

1   *Population trends 4th quarter*, Statistics Netherlands, 2006.

'Protective wraps' offers a different, new perspective in the practice of care. Rather than, by definition, replacing the old familiar practice, it offers an added conceptual framework to the regular way of working. In many cases, it helps to look at youth issues from a different angle. More from the perspective of the client, from the family context and with a view to the migration history. That does not mean that the usual methodologies should be abandoned. But it does mean that creativity is sometimes required to make things fit. You must be flexible and in some cases be able to park your old beliefs for a while. Occasionally you will also have to be prepared to look for unorthodox solutions to certain problems. In this final chapter, we will recall all the ingredients of the model. We will reflect on how the basic principles relate to regular thinking in healthcare. What does it mean in practice that the relationship with the client is important, and that you as a care worker must be able to commit a personal part of yourself? Can you give shape to continuity in care in the current system? What unorthodox solutions can you think of? And how does the model relate to methods such as 'Family Network Consultation', the 'Solution-oriented Approach' and 'Signs of Safety'?

All the elements of the model in a row

After migration from Suriname to the Netherlands, Kitlyn Tjin A Djie discovered that her family history and structure were totally different from the way families are organized in the Netherlands. She also found that the care sector does not deal adequately with the different context of migrants. During her work as a transcultural systemic therapist, she discovered theoretical concepts that support her ideas. We will now list the most important aspects of 'Protective wraps'.

'Protective wraps'

'Protective wraps' is the essence of the story. 'Protective wraps' consists of two nouns. 'Protective wraps' are the safe wrappings that you as a care worker can offer your client. This can be family, or something that is a reminder of it. But it can also be old habits, traditions, food, home furnishings, smells; in short, anchors that remind people of the familiar ways of the past. 'Protective wraps' can also be used to form a verb. You can protectively wrap your client, by helping to look for those wrappings and anchors. By protectively wrapping your clients, you offer them the opportunity to compose themselves in a vulnerable life transition phase. Because the familiar ways of the old days provide the strength to step into the uncertain future.

Families

It is important to know that there is a distinction between families from a collective system and families from an individual system. The purpose of children who grow up in the individual system is to develop themselves and to become happy. The purpose of children from a collective family system is to contribute to the continuity of the family. Families carry strengths within them that can be harnessed for the wellbeing of the child. It is a blind spot that families over three or four generations together shape solutions to problems.

Migration

Migrants from collective systems frequently experience major emotional consequences as a result of migration. Migration makes the purpose of shaping family continuity a lot more difficult to fulfill. In addition, the entire set-up of the support and decision-making structure changes, and new strategies must be found to deal with life phase transitions such as death, birth and unemployment. The impact of migration is a blind spot for both the migrant and the Dutch care worker. It is important to dwell on this.

Intercultural competencies

Because your own background influences your reaction to the Other, it is important to have a clear idea about your own cultural baggage. How is your family structured, what are the important messages you had instilled in you? But also: what is your culture, your history? Then it is important to develop a deeper understanding of the other person. What does the family look like, is it a collective or an individual system? What are the facts about its migration history? What are the views on parenting? Who are the figures of authority in the family? You must know your own sensibilities, your sacred cows. Once you know which ones they are, they don't have to stand in the way of an open dialogue. Because you can put them aside for a while. To enable you to switch perspectives. To look at the situation from the reality of the other person. Be constantly aware of blind spots in communication. Hidden dimensions cannot always be cleared up.

Instruments

The most important instrument for discovering your own cultural baggage and that of others is the genogram. By drawing a genogram together with your client, and while doing that asking questions aimed at the context and not at the individual, you get a good picture of the structure and history of the family. You will also see where the strengths and weaknesses are hidden in the system. Through making the genogram, clients can tell their story, which in itself has a healing effect. Other instruments are the lifeline, the use of contextual questions, the TOPOI model, the life story, and 'testimony'.

What distinguishes 'Protective wraps'?

'Protective wraps' distinguishes itself from many regular Dutch care methods because it adds and combines a number of constructive aspects.
- As a care worker, you focus on the multi-generation family system and you don't limit yourself to the nuclear family system.
- As a care worker, you align with your client's perspective; you follow the ideas and the solutions of families and you continue by exchanging your own personal and professional perspective with the family.
- As a care worker, you don't know, but ask.
- As a care worker, you don't help, but you facilitate the self-reliance capacity of the system.
- You contribute a personal story, instead of distancing yourself in the relationship.
- You use your own story to interpret differences that you encounter in the dialogue with the other person, instead of limiting yourself to the similarities.
- How does 'Protective wraps' relate to the Dutch views on care?

Dominant discourse

People's actions and thinking are strongly influenced by the dominant discourse in society.[1] People are 'framed' between important views. That's the way we always do it, and if you do it differently, you lose the connection. People have to toe the line all the time. Care workers are often influenced by the dominant discourse in the Netherlands in the field of healthcare, namely the intrapsychic thinking focused on the individual person. Another example of this is that bringing your personal story into the relationship with the client is considered unprofessional. The dominant discourse in the Dutch care sector is sometimes at odds with the principles of 'Protective wraps'. If you are not aware of this, you will no longer be able to reflect, or to switch perspectives. Then that's the end of the dialogue. An important advice for care workers is to look for the dominant discourse in society in relation to your client. Which experiences, beliefs or habits of your client end up in the margin, are not heard, pushed aside, because they don't fit in here? These can be issues such as arranged marriages, rituals and the way of experiencing religion. Or the view that all migrants should be able to speak Dutch. It is important to be aware of these and to give them space, so that trust and openness are allowed to exist. The extent to which you act according to the dominant discourse in the Dutch care sector is also important. Because you will have to park these sacred cows too for the time being, in order to be able to work with 'Protective wraps'.

---

1   Freedman, J. en G. Combs (1996), 'Shifting paradigms: From systems to stories.' In: Freedman, J. and G. Combs, *Narrative Therapy: The social construction of preferred realities*, chapter 1. New York: Norton.

The relationship

Youth care workers often think that they need a lot of time to build a relationship with the client. Now that Bureau Jeugdzorg has become a second-line institution, the case managers are no longer allowed to provide care. On the basis of an examination, they have to give advice on the type of care that is likely to be the most effective. To this end, they are allowed a limited number of interviews. In their perception they are no longer allowed to build a relationship, due to lack of time. However, that is a misapprehension. You don't need all that much time to build a relationship. When you work with 'Protective wraps', you have an excellent basis for building a good working relationship with the client within a very short time. Because if you are able to quickly immerse yourself in the history and context of the other person by making a genogram, asking contextual questions, switching your perspective to that of the client and communicating about that, you will have a constructive working relationship within a few hours. In this connection it is important to take the resolving capacity of the client's family system as a starting point. That system has presumably always worked, but now it is faltering somewhere. As a care worker, you try to find out where it goes wrong. Next, you make it possible for the system to work again. In the process, you constantly keep switching perspectives and, if necessary, you also communicate your own perspective, without denouncing the other person's perspective. So, you shouldn't be afraid to commit a personal part of yourself. You can assume that by doing so you will establish a functional working relationship. There is absolutely no need for building a dependent relationship. You are a facilitator, not a savior. You facilitate the self-resolving capacity of the system. In that you are important. And for that you don't need all that much time.

In the multicultural society that is the Netherlands, it is impossible to come up with a blueprint for a solution to a problem. There is such a great diversity of backgrounds, histories, cultures and habits. As a care worker, you just can't know anymore. It is becoming more and more common for care workers to adopt the 'Not Knowing Position'[2]. That ties in well with 'Protective wraps'. However, what is absolutely not common, what is even a taboo in the care sector, is you bringing a personal part into the professional relationship. Nevertheless, there are several reasons in favor of doing so. First, in the introduction to chapter 7 we saw that the relationship between care worker and client is the most effective aspect in the care contact. Research shows that 70% of a successful conclusion results from the contact. Only 10% can be attributed to the method.[3] So it would seem that it makes no difference at all which method you use. As a guideline for yourself, it is of course useful to choose one. It is important that you are a warm person for your client. You can achieve this by being open and by telling a personal story every now and then. This creates a personal contact, which makes the client trust you. The second

---

2   Anderson, H. and H. Goolishian (1992), 'The Client is the Expert: a Not-Knowing Approach to Therapy'. In: S. McNamee and K. Gergen (Eds.), *Therapy as social construction*, pp. 25-39. London: Sage.
3   Clark, M.D. (2001), 'Change-focussed Youth Work', *Journal of the Center for Families, Children and the Courts*.

reason is that by telling stories yourself, you invite others to tell their story as well. When you tell a single mother from Ethiopia, "Here single mothers always do it this way. They are supported by so and so, but they frequently have a very difficult time because, with us, the families are not by definition there for them. My sister, for example..." Then you ask the single mother how that used to be for her and how it is now. In this way you have given her a good and safe platform on which to present her story. The closer you stick to yourself, the safer it becomes. If you tell a story about yourself or about your family, it becomes easier for the other person to tell a personal story as well. Thus, you can apply the personal part professionally. After all, you facilitate the relationship with it. Moreover, you can safeguard the professional within you when it is time to alternate the personal with the professional again. It is important to enter the relationship with your heart, but you must be very alert when doing so.

Service department employee Theo talks about his experience with applying personal aspects in care contacts.

> *"Apart from advantages this way of working also has disadvantages. There is a risk, particularly with families that are not so strong. Just like that you've become a walking source of information, your assistance is called in for everything. That's also what happened to me. That for ages I had been on a different location with a different job, but that I was still telephoned by a client because things wouldn't work with that other institution. Or on behalf of a child who couldn't find an internship. One mother even wanted to involve me in the purchase of a dog! Before you know it, you have become a part of the system yourself. You're working with people on the basis of a relationship, and in the world of care that is a point of discussion. About professional distance and that kind of thing. I never had much of a problem with it myself. Perhaps you should be a little clearer about what you are there for, and that there are other people for other things."*

In this example we see that Theo at the back of his mind still has the idea that he is acting unprofessionally by more or less merging with the system. In individually functioning systems, the so-called I-oriented systems, it may indeed be inappropriate to become a part of the system, but in collective family systems it is an advantage. Because those systems themselves provide psychosocial care. In order to get a faltering system back on track there, it is necessary to temporarily become a figure of support or authority, or an anchor. It is good to be aware of the fact that the family puts you in that place because they trust you. If you're concerned about being called upon 24 hours per day, you can make it clear that you like to be part of the family system, but Monday to Friday, 9am to 5pm.

Continuity

Although it seems an impossible task in the current system, it is nevertheless important to focus on continuity for clients. Healthcare in the Netherlands is extremely fragmented. The first care worker to turn up is allowed to have three interviews, then comes the next one, who is allowed five. Subsequently, the Help at Home version 'Families First' begins, which is allowed to last six weeks, the next form of care is allowed for eight months, and on it goes. It is disastrous for people with a migration history and a fragmented family structure to encounter so much discontinuity in the care system. Children with a migration history, who have already suffered so many losses in their family, are moved from care worker to care worker, and from shelter to shelter. In a family a father may be depressed, a mother has gynecological problems, one child has behavioral problems at home and another child keeps skipping school. In the Netherlands, it is certainly not inconceivable that all the members of the family are provided with a different care worker and a different kind of care. Whereas in fact it's about one and the same complaint. Perhaps the complaint is about homesickness, or about the loss of a protective wrap, of embedment. But all those people receive a different kind of treatment at a different location. That drives people from a collective system crazy. The dominant view in the Netherlands that everything should be efficient and cheap has caused the effects of this to remain a hidden dimension. So, if you as a care worker see an opportunity to contribute to continuity in care, seize it with both hands, in the interest of the client.

Theo speaking again:

> *"The care sector is becoming increasingly remote from people. More and more barriers are being raised. It's not intentional, but still. I have always found that one interview at someone's home yields a lot more than three interviews at the office. Because you can see how someone lives, whether it's a hyperactive child.*
> *When you see that it is a messy environment, you can imagine why the child is hyperactive. In this way you also learn, for example, that the grandmother still plays an important role. Anyway, Bureau Jeugdzorg Drenthe is a second-line organization. There is a filter for Bureau Jeugdzorg already. Bureau Jeugdzorg is to decide whether someone can be accepted as a client, i.e. whether there are serious problems. This has to do with operational management. There should be no waiting lists, the flow should simply remain high. So, efficiency is examined. What is the best way, how can we limit travel time, so that care workers can see as many clients as possible? Those kinds of considerations play a role. That makes it difficult to go and visit people. To relax, have a cup of coffee and talk about their situation. I will keep arguing the case for that."*

Organizations can be creative in pushing the boundaries of their possibilities. What an organization can strive for in an attempt to achieve continuity in care is for each new form of care, from intake up to and including completion of the process, link the same care worker to the form of care involved. This requires care workers to be broadly oriented and not too specialized.[4] If you consider the fact that the relationship is more important than the method, the picture is complete. Because

---

4   Stoelinga, B. (2001), *Naar een brede professionaliteit. De wensen en behoeften van de klant als uitgangspunt.* Maatwerk 2.

the provision of care will be more efficient and more effective in less time, so the cost to society will be considerably lower.

Unorthodox solutions

Looking for solutions in the context of the client sometimes requires an uncommon approach. For example, it is important to call in a Winti expert if a Surinamese family indicates a need for one. Muslim children with psychiatric disorders may benefit from Islamic healers. People from Africa can be helped by certain herbs for specific problems. De Jong[5] has conducted comparative research into the effects of local and Western medicine in case of psychosocial complaints. Research in Burundi shows that local healers are more successful in treating psychosocial problems than academic or Western forms of care. Cees Wierda, director of Bureau Jeugdzorg Drenthe, found that as a Westerner he benefited more from the treatment by a traditional doctor in Ghana than from the antibiotics he had brought with him. An infection on his leg worsened to such an extent after taking the antibiotics course, that he turned to a medicine man from the village. He put some leaves on the wound and after four days it was cured. We learn from this that you cannot always believe in one truth.

Kitlyn:

> *I asked a female refugee who had problems with her daughter, who in her village was allowed to interfere with mother-daughter relationships.*
> *She said: "In my village it was an old wise woman." I asked her: "Am I like that for you here?" She laughed at me. She said: "No, you're not. But you can find her for me here." She indicated that it should be someone with magnetizing powers. So, I put an older Reiki master on her path.* [6]

This mother had previously consulted a native Dutch care worker. She told him what she needed. She could see in his eyes that he was trying to fit her into a category familiar to him. But nothing in his toolkit could be applied to her. That made him lose contact and she opted out. In order to be of help to migrants it is important to first look together at how problems are solved in the country of origin. Then together you can search for equivalents here. Otherwise you will irrevocably lose the dialogue.

Intercultural project member Jeanne talks about a case:

> *A client of mine, a girl from Africa, was severely traumatized by her flight history. Her mother could no longer handle her, she was expelled from various schools, and is now under family guardianship. She has absolutely no control over her emotions. I think she*

---

5   Jong, J. de, see abstract: www.integralepsychiatrie.nl/nl/lezingen, 2006.
6   Drenthe was first in the Netherlands to develop an initiative in which all the possibilities for psychosocial care are presented as a combined package on one website, www.hulpindrenthe.nl. Both regular and alternative care offered are to be found here, so it is easy for care workers to look for alternative forms of care.

has an odd look in her eyes, like she is possessed. Her mother confirmed that, she keeps changing, like something is coming over her. The girl herself also said that it seemed as if someone else was living inside her. I then thought of Suriname. In Suriname there are traditional doctors. And if something is the matter with you like with this girl, it's often because something is wrong in the family. Because someone has done something wrong. Or your ancestors. In such cases all kinds of rituals have to be performed for your mind to start functioning again, for you to regain your balance. So I asked that mother, what would you do in Africa if you were in this situation with your daughter. She told me that there she would indeed go to a traditional healer. She opened up completely. So, now I am looking for someone to help her here, in the Netherlands. **"**

How does 'Protective wraps' relate to regular approaches in care?

Methods embraced by Bureau Jeugdzorg Drenthe in recent years are the 'Family Network Consultation', the 'Solution-oriented Approach' and 'Signs of Safety'. All these methods reflect the demand-oriented trend in the world of care. We will shed light on the extent to which these methods are consistent with 'Protective wraps' and the consequences for the practical usability.

'Family gatherings'

The 'Family Network Consultation' is one of the care methods applied by Bureau Jeugdzorg Drenthe. The Consultation is facilitated by a care worker, who also decides who qualifies for it. A variant is the 'Own Force Conference.'[7] This is not a care method, but a decision-making model in which the family comes to agreements about what is needed. This is facilitated by an independent person. Care can be one of the outcomes to be included in the plan. These methods are based on the wisdom and the cultural thinking of Maoris in New Zealand. They discovered that their children's situation and complaints worsened when they came into contact with Western care. They then offered their own way of approaching problems to the regular care institutions, whereby the family draws up a problem-solving plan for the care workers. The method originates from the collective systems thinking. As far as we know, it is the only care concept from an ethnic people that has been embraced in the Western world. In New Zeeland it is now even included in the law that the (extended) family is primarily responsible for the care and protection of a child. The same law also ensures that families must be protected and supported in order to be able to optimally fulfill this task.[8] Unfortunately, in the Netherlands there is a still a long way to go in this respect. The family gatherings tie in well with 'Protective wraps' because the supportive, corrective and resolving powers of the family are utilized. On the other hand, it is important to realize that in the Netherlands, there are no migrant

---

7   See www.eigen-kracht.nl.
8   Worrall, J. (2005), *Grandparents Raising Grandchildren: A handbook for grandparents and other kin givers.* Grandparents Raising Grandchildren Trust Auckland Boughtwood Printing House.

families that function in a tribal context like the Maoris. On the contrary, they tend to be battered systems whereby important people had to be left behind in the country of origin. When applying family meetings in the Netherlands, the first thing should be to look for forgotten problem-solving strategies of the family by using 'Protective wraps'. Only then can a family conference be effective.

'Solution-oriented Approach'

The 'Solution-oriented Approach' focuses on solutions instead of on problems.[9] In doing so, it tries to relate to the ideas of the client about the future and what could be changed for the better in the future. It is based on the belief that people, despite the problems they experience in life, possess qualities that enable them to bring about positive changes. Therefore, just like 'Protective wraps', the 'Solution-oriented approach' is based on the inherent strength of systems. In both cases, following the ideas of the family is the focal point. That is why both approaches can be excellently applied at the same time, provided that, in the 'Solution-oriented Approach', extended families and figures of authority come into the picture. A complementary aspect to the 'Solution-oriented Approach' is that with 'Protective wraps' insight into the history of the client is crucial. Current problems are frequently related to outstanding issues from the past. Moreover, problem-solving strategies can often be found by connecting forgotten memories to the here and now.[10] People are often no longer aware of their problem-solving strategies, and rediscover them in their memory once they are immersed in family, the culture, the religion, anchors from the past.

The 'Solution-oriented Approach' believes that there is no need for a relationship between solutions and problems.[11] In order to be able to connect both approaches, which certainly is a potential possibility, the importance of the past should also be recognized in the 'Solution-oriented Approach'.

'Signs of Safety'

'Signs of Safety'[12] is a method aimed at the development and implementation of a safety plan. The plan incorporates the concerns and dangers as well as the strengths and powerful features in the family. It is particularly suitable when there is a threat of imminent danger. It is focused on the creation of partnerships with parents and children, being honest about what needs to be changed and taking into account the perspective of parents, without losing sight of what is necessary for a safe situation. 'Signs of Safety' uses the protective powers of a system. A dominant view in the Netherlands is that we tend to look at what is missing, what is wrong, what is not

---

9   Jong, P. de and I. Berg (2001), 'Co-Constructing Cooperation with Mandated Clients', *Social Work*, 46, pp. 361-375.
10 Ramdas, A. (1992), 'Heimwee'. In: A. Ramdas, *De papegaai, de stier en de klimmende bougainvillea*, essays. De Bezige Bij.
11 Shazer, S. de (1991), *Putting difference to work*. New York: Norton.
12 Turnell, A. and S. Edwards (1999), *Signs Of Safety: a solution and safety oriented approach to child protection*. New York: WW Norton.

yet in order. While 'Signs of Safety' looks at what is already there, what people can do and what they do. Traditionally, examinations in cases of care notifications are focused exclusively on the threatening factors, and there is blindness to latent resources. Such as a grandfather, a grandmother, an uncle or an aunt who in the past has proven to be important for the safety of the child in question. It is important to know that in principle all parents would like to be the best educators of their child, but sometimes they temporarily just cannot fulfill that role. The principles of 'Signs of Safety' tie in well with 'Protective wraps'.

Family gatherings, the 'Solution-oriented Approach' and 'Signs of Safety' are all system-oriented, demand-oriented and based on the strengths of the system. When applying these methods, elements of 'Protective wraps' can be added in order to open up hidden layers, so that you get the best of both worlds. Collaboration will then lead to synergy, to something greater than the sum of its parts.

How does 'Protective wraps' relate to the requirements of new style welfare?

The current pillars of society in the field of welfare are protection, self-sufficiency, participation, caring for each other and social cohesion. In 2011, the government presented eight beacons that together should give substance and direction to a more collective, more professional and more efficient organization of social support. The youth professional is expected to mobilize the client's own strengths. That ties in seamlessly with protective wraps. After all, protective wraps advocates looking for and utilizing families' own strengths. Per beacon we will indicate where this touches upon protective wraps.[13]

Beacon 1. Be focused on the questions behind the demand

Many methods and interventions aim to be demand-oriented, but nevertheless run the risk of reasoning from the perspective of what's on offer. Before you know it, you have stuck a label on the family, and with the method championed by your organization you already have the format for the care to be provided in mind. The procedure is ready and only needs to be applied.

'Focusing on demand' is a rhetorical trap. People seeking care usually do not have a clear question; they have a complaint or a problem situation, caused by an accumulation of factors, rooted in history and in the generations, spread across multiple areas of life. To want to reduce this problem to one question implies a one-dimensional way of operating instead of approaching the problem systemically.

The regular one-dimensional, intrapsychic approach can easily lead to an unconscious bias on the part of the professional, who is out of his depth on account of the complexity of the issues and the diversity among citizens in a multicultural society. To get away from this, it is important to go back to the Not Knowing

---

13   Tjin A Djie, K. en I. Zwaan (2012), 'Beschermjassen als baken voor intercultureel werken, Mobiliseren van de eigen oplossingsstrategieën van familiesystemen'. In: M. Berk, K. Verhaar, A. Hoogenboom et al. (eds.), *De jeugdprofessional in ontwikkeling*. Kluwer.

Position, as described earlier in this chapter. After all, as a professional you cannot know the family's own problem-solving strategies. The family is the expert in the field of solutions that have worked in the system.

Beacon 2. Mobilize the citizen's own strength

Families are focused on survival, on continuity. An entire family apparatus – including grandparents, uncles and aunts – is committed to bringing up the children. Organizing psychosocial support is highly developed in we-oriented family systems. If there is a problem in the family, if someone develops complaints, the system will make all kinds of efforts. Old rituals are dusted off, family members are called upon. And if that doesn't work, professional care comes into the picture.

In Dutch families, too, there are important figures of support and authority outside the nuclear family, who can play a role in the decision-making process and the approach to the problem situation. In addition to family, think of neighbors and friends of the parents.

If as a professional you are unaware of this mechanism, you will be unable to see it. The most important assignment, therefore, is to be aware of this from the very first contact and to pay attention to it. It often happens that, due to the migration history, the we-oriented family apparatus is no longer the well-oiled machine it used to be. In those cases it is important for a professional, together with the parents, to look for ways to restore continuity.

Beacon 3. Direct approach

If, due to violations of privacy and self-determination, it is not possible to reach citizens who are in need of care and assistance, the so-called care avoiders, you can go in search of contact points in the system of the person or the family concerned. From the perspective of Western I-oriented values, this would seem improper, because you are acting without the person's knowledge. However, it is proper for protective wraps and for collective systems, because you are seeking the strength and connection in the familiar environment of the person.

Beacon 4. Formal and informal

In line with new style welfare as well as with protective wraps, the professional should exercise restraint. The professional aims to address and reinforce the self-governing ability of the citizens. It is pointed out by the government that informal assistance in that respect can be found through social networks, voluntary organizations and neighborhood associations. Protective wraps adds an informal source of strength to this: the family perspective. While it may well be the greatest source of strength, the family is often overlooked by professionals socialized in an individualistic system.

The biggest obstacle for harnessing the strength offered by family systems is often the professional himself. Unintentionally, of course; it's simply a blind spot.

Beacon 5. Careful balance between collective and individual solutions

Collective solutions connect seamlessly with clients from family systems that are not focused on the individual but on the collective. A family meeting, a collective eating facility, a training course on parenting in the Netherlands, these are all activities in which embedment in group and culture can be used as a source of strength.

Beacon 6. Integrated approach

For an integrated approach to problems in a family, it is important to safeguard continuity. Families with problems have frequently experienced so much discontinuity in their history, that it is harmful if more is added on top of that. It requires that you as a professional remain in control and that you switch between different contexts. But you should make sure – where possible – that the care seeker deals with the same person whenever possible, even if multiple institutions or facilities are concerned. In a transcultural systemic approach, focusing on continuity is a greater good than focusing on the question.

Beacon 7. Not noncommittal but result-oriented

This principle concerns agreements about who does what. What kind of support from the professional can you count on as a care seeker, and what should be your own contribution as a care seeker? A blind spot here is the in-between space: the relationship between the professional and the care seeker. An important condition in protective wraps for being able to provide effective care, is that the relationship is a central point. Now that you know that seventy per cent of a successful conclusion of a care contact can be attributed to the relationship, you can imagine that the person within you as a professional is of vital importance.

Beacon 8. Room for the professional

We have seen that working with protective wraps sometimes requires an unorthodox approach. After all, using solutions and strategies in the context of the client can lead to an approach that is rarely accepted in Western thinking. Religious rituals, local remedies, traditional herbalists, magical healers... Yet this helps care seekers in being embedded in their own culture, so that they can regain their strength.

Working with more than two generations in families, and not just with the nuclear family, also touches upon the sacred cows of individual thinking. But for families from collective systems, the family approach is the only logical step in dealing with difficult situations.

Room for the professional means that sufficient room is provided to do what is necessary, what works. That sacred cows in the Dutch care system can be left for what they are, and multiple perspectives and multiple truths can be applied.

The organization as 'Protective wrap'

The active ingredients from 'Protective wraps' should also be supported by managers in the internal organization. This not only means that they give you as a care worker room to apply them, but also that they can be found in their own leadership style. You can't provide a client with optimal protective wraps if you yourself are not enveloped in a protective wrap by your superior, your team, the management and the organization as a whole. You should be facilitated in examining your own story, be allowed to park your sacred cows, to look for unorthodox solutions, et cetera. Since 'Protective wraps' is sometimes at odds with regular methods, this will not happen automatically.

For an organization it is important to develop a workforce that reflects diversity. To obtain and maintain such diversity, it is also important to envelop employees in 'protective wraps'. However, it would go too far to enter into detail here. That subject deserves its own book! And meanwhile we have written that book. *Managing diversity in the workplace* deals with how to give shape to safety, diversity and productivity in the workplace by using protective wraps.[14]

Sankofa

The fact that 'Protective wraps' is nothing new but has been borne along in the collective memory of families and peoples for centuries, is evident from the metaphor Sankofa from Ghana. Sankofa is a bird and also a concept from the Akan, a language of Ghana. It means that we can go back to the past to retrieve what we have forgotten. Sanko means 'go back' and fa means 'take'. Sankofa is a bird that moves forward while looking back. A fine symbol for 'Protective wraps'.

[14] Tjin A Djie, K. en I. Zwaan (2010), *Managen van diversiteit op de werkvloer*. Assen: Koninklijke Van Gorcum.

Assignment

- Write down which lessons from this book you mean to put in practice; what would you like to hold on to and not forget for the future?
- Suppose you had a magic wand: what would you change in the professional practice of your discipline?

Word of thanks

This book was realized in a positive flow of energy. We had all the winds in our sails. Everyone involved in the project made a positive contribution through enthusiasm, faith, openness, commitment, drive and passion. We were weaving a rug, which was a pleasant process. Now we are rolling out the rug and thank everyone who supported this process, directly or indirectly. There are a number of persons in particular we would like to thank.

Ina Kuipers, Ine van Diepstraten and Peter Strijbosch because they are the founders of the project at Bureau Jeugdzorg Drenthe. Ellen Meijer, because she contributed to the foundations from the very beginning. Cees Wierda, director and project manager, because he committed himself to the project in a special way. Nelly Everts, for the coordinating and facilitating role she played. The project staff members Ahmed el Hag, Joan Wolthers and Carlijn Molewater, because they were instrumental in promoting 'Protective wraps' in the care sector and the organization, with a continuous show of positivism and enthusiasm. And Marlon Levens for his enthusiastic participation. All those who were interviewed for their sensitive, candid, personal, vulnerable stories. It is so special that they are willing to share their stories so that others can discover their own. Without their stories, this book could not have been written.

The regular 'co-readers'. We thank Dirck van Bekkum, anthropologist, for his extensive and very encouraging contributions, particularly to the fourth and fifth chapters. Marjon Arends, transcultural systemic therapist, has helped to get to the heart of matters, particularly in the sixth and seventh chapters. Karin Zwaan, journalist, cracked critical notes on crooked sentences, unnecessary jargon, and helped to make the text as attractive as possible. Mariele Mijnlieff, adviser, applied her analytical and critical mind to the context of care.

Corrie van de Ven, project assistant, was not only a gifted proofreader, but facilitated to perfection all the incidental issues with regard to the process of writing the book. Resy Broekhoven, regional manager Spirit Amsterdam South East, nuanced certain views expressed in the eight chapter. Marieke Brenninkmeijer, higher education lecturer, has read and commented on the book from the perspective of Higher Vocational Education. Liesbeth Orsel, secretary, has enthusiastically dotted the i's and crossed the t's in the text.

Additionally, we thank for their support and feedback: Titia Struiving, Bart Deuss, Jane Tjin A Djie, Nienke Jaarsma, Fariba Rhmaty, and Martha Beijert.

Robin Fiolet, thank you for the beautiful cover illustration, and George Schriemer, thank you for the striking image of Sankofa. Jaap Hoeksma, thank you for the wonderful poem that spontaneously arose in your head when you met Kitlyn at the greengrocer's.

Finally, Kitlyn thanks her family for the beautiful stories that brought her where she is today.

Kitlyn Tjin A Djie and Irene Zwaan

About the authors

Kitlyn Tjin A Djie is a transcultural systemic therapist and trainer. She developed the protective wraps model in response to the linear Western white individual-oriented thinking in youth care. She is the owner of Bureau Beschermjassen (Protective Wraps Agency) and offers training and education on the application of Protective Wraps in care, education and the welfare sector.

Her professions and initiatives are as diverse as her background. She prefers to commute between different contexts. In cultures, in families, in languages, in generations... Through her work, she intends to facilitate adults and children to understand each other. Her ideal is for every child to have access to what is needed to grow up well. That is why, together with children and adults, she goes in search of a language through which they can understand each other. That language is not only to be found in the head, but also in the soul, the body, the spirit and the family.

Together with Zwaan, she wrote a number of books and articles about Protective Wraps. An overview of publications is provided on the website.

www.beschermjassen.nl
info@beschermjassen.nl

Irene Zwaan is a development sociologist and writer, and has expertise in the field of emancipation and diversity. She publishes on inclusion and exclusion mechanisms in society. Together with Tjin A Djie she is working on the development and description of the Protective Wraps model.

www.irenezwaan.nl

Literature

Note: all titles have been translated to English to give readers a better idea of the source materials that were used. The English translation is mentioned in between brackets. However, not all publications are available in English.

Anderson, H. en H. Goolishian (1992), 'The Client is the Expert: a Not-Knowing Approach to Therapy'. In: S. McNamee en K. Gergen (eds.), *Therapy as social construction*, pp. 25-39, London: Sage.
Arends, A.M. (1998), 'Het ondergesneeuwde lichaam' ('The submerged body'), *Tijdschrift voor Sociale Psychiatrie (Journal for Social Psychiatry)*, 51, pp. 13-25.
Bakker, H., 'Iedereen heeft beschermjassen nodig' ('Everyone needs protective wraps'), interview with K. Tjin A Djie in *Vrouw en Gezondheid (Woman and Health)*, November/December 1997.
Bekkum, D. van (2004), 'Nederlandse identiteit als basis voor burgerschap – een antropologische visie' ('Dutch identity as a basis for citizenship – an anthropological vision'), *Civis Mundi*, January.
Bekkum, D. van, M. van de Ende, S. Heezen en A. Hijmans van den Bergh (1996), '"Migratie als Transitie" De liminele kwetsbaarheid van migranten en vluchtelingen' ('"Migration as Transition" The liminal vulnerability of migrants and refugees'). In: J. de Jong en M. v.d. Berg (eds.), *Handboek Transculturele Psychiatrie en Psychotherapie (Manual Transcultural Psychiatry and Psychotherapy)*. Lisse.
Bekkum, D. van, G.O. Helberg, K. Tjin A Djie en I. Zwaan (2010), 'Rituelen en beschermjassen' ('Rituals and protective wraps'). In: J. de Jong en S. Colijn (eds.), *Handboek culturele psychiatrie en psychotherapie (Manual Transcultural Psychiatry and Psychotherapy)*. Utrecht: De Tijdstroom.
Boedjarath, I. en D. van Bekkum (eds.) (1997), *Een blik in de transculturele hulpverlening, 15 jaar ervaring met verlies en verrijking (An insight into transcultural care, 15 years of experience with loss and enrichment)*. Utrecht: Van Arkel.
Bohlmeijer, E. (2007), 'Herinneringen, levensverhalen en gezondheid' ('Memories, life stories and health'). In: E. Bohlmeijer, L. Mies en G. Westerhof, *De betekenis van levensverhalen, theoretische beschouwingen en toepassingen in onderzoek en praktijk (The meaning of life stories, theoretical considerations and application in research and practice)*, pp. 31-39. Houten: Bohn Stafleu van Loghum.
Bourdieu, P. (2001), *Masculine domination*. Cambridge: Polity Press.
Brinkgreve, C. (2014), *Vertel, over de kracht van verhalen (Tell me! About the power of stories)*. Atlas Contact.
Clark, M.D. (2001), 'Change-focussed Youth Work', *Journal of the Center for Families, Children and the Courts*.
Crul, M. et al. (2013), *Superdiversiteit (Superdiversity)*, Elitesproject.eu.
Cuyvers, P. (2006), 'The Netherlands: tolerance and traditionalism'. In: James Georgas, John W. Berry, Fons J.R. van de Vijver, Cigdem Kagitçibasi and Ype H. Poortinga (eds.), *Families across cultures. A 30 Nation Psychological study*, pp. 410-419. Cambridge: Cambridge University Press.
Dijk, J. van en B. Schreuder (2001), 'De getuigenis als therapie. Beschrijving van een kortdurende therapeutische methode voor getraumatiseerde slachtoffers van politiek geweld' ('The testimony as therapy. Description of a short-term therapeutical method for traumatised victims of political violence'), *Tijdschrift voor Psychotherapie (Journal for Psychotherapy)*, 27.

Dijkstra, P.A., *Het zit in de familie (It's all in the family)*. Oration on the occasion of the acceptance of the chair of Relationship Demographics at the University of Utrecht, 29 October 2003.

Dijkstra, P. en A. Komter (2004), 'Hoe zien Nederlandse families eruit?' ('What do Dutch families look like?') *DEMOS*, vol. 20, nr. 10.

Dijkstra, P. en H. de Valk (2007), 'Criminelen in de familie, Verband tussen crimineel gedrag en bevolkingskenmerken onderzocht' ('Criminals in the family, Investigation of connection between criminal behavior and population characteristics'), *DEMOS*, vol. 23, nr. 1.

Does, M. van den en A. Arce (1998), 'The value of narratives in rural development projects. A case from Equador', *Journal of agricultural education and extension*, vol. 5, nr. 2, pp. 85-98.

Ende, M. van den en A. Savenije (2002), 'Zwijgen versus spreken, Geheimen als copingsmechanismen bij bi-culturele adolescenten' ('Silence versus speech, Secrets as coping mechanisms among bicultural adolescents'), *Tijdschrift voor systeemtherapie (Journal for System Therapy)*, nr. 14, pp. 229-243.

Foorthuis, W.R. en P. Brood (eds.) (2002), *Gids voor cultuur en landschap (Guide to culture and nature)*. Uitgeverij DE PLOEG.

Freedman, J. en G. Combs (1996), 'Shifting paradigms: From systems to stories.' In: Freedman, J. en G. Combs, *Narrative Therapy: The social construction of preferred realities*, chapter 1. New York: Norton.

Geldof, D. (2015), *Superdiversiteit, hoe migratie onze samenleving verandert (Superdiversity, how migration changes our society)*. Leuven: Acco.

Geldof, D. et al. (2015), *Transmigratie, hulp verlenen in een wereld van superdiversiteit (Transmigration, providing care in a world of superdiversity)*. Leuven: Acco.

Ghorashi, H., 'Is de tijd rijp voor reflectie op integratievraagstukken?' ('Is the time ripe for reflection on integration issues?'). *D66 magazine Thema Idee (Theme Idea)*, September 2006.

Gibson, F.M.A. (2004), *The past in present: Using reminiscence in health and social care*. London: Health Professions Press.

Girigori, O. J. (2015). *Father Absence: The consequences for reproductive behavior and mating strategies among females*. Rijksuniversiteit Groningen.

Gowricharn, R. (2001), 'In- en uitsluiting in Nederland. Een overzicht van empirische bevindingen' ('Inclusion and exclusion in the Netherlands. An overview of empirical findings'); study Wetenschappelijke Raad voor het Regeringsbeleid (Scientific Council for Government Policy), Rijswijk.

Groeneveld, L., 'Voel je senang in een beschermjas' ('Feeling happy in a protective wrap'), interview with K. Tjin A Djie in *Contrast*, maart 2007.

Hoffman, E. en F. Ogunc-Serap (1996), 'Interculturele gespreksvoering' ('Intercultural interviewing'). In: J. de Jong en M. van den Berg (eds.), *Transculturele Psychiatrie & Psychotherapie (Transcultural Psychiatry & Psychotherapy), handboek voor hulpverlening en beleid*. Swets & Zeitling publishers.

Hoffman, E. (2002), *Interculturele gespreksvoering. Theorie en praktijk van het TOPOI-model (Intercultural interviewing. Theory and practice of the TOPOI model)*. Houten: Bohn Stafleu van Loghum.

Hondius, D., 'Gemengde huwelijken, gemengde gevoelens' ('Mixed marriages, mixed feelings'), *DEMOS*, vol. 19, August 2003.

Hooft, L., 'Collega's met familietrekjes. Hoe gezinspatronen zich herhalen op je werk' ('Colleagues with family traits. How family patterns repeat themselves at work'), *VB Magazine*, December 1998.

Hout, A. van en K. Tjin A Djie (2007), 'Van hulpverlening naar zelfredzaamheid' ('From aid to independence'). In: S. Spinder, L. Joanknecht, A. van Hout en R. van Pagée (eds.), *Krachten en Kansen, Initiatieven voor vernieuwing in zorg en welzijn (Powers and Chances, Initiatives for innovations in heathcare)*. Bohn Stafleu van Loghum.

Huis, M. van en L. Steenhof (2004), 'Echtscheidingskansen van allochtonen in Nederland' ('Divorce risks for migrants in the Netherlands'), *Bevolking en gezin (Population and family)*, 33, 2, pp. 127-154.

Jessurun, C.M. (1994), 'Genogrammen en etniciteit' ('Genograms and ethnicity'). In: J. Hoogsteder (ed.), *Etnocentrisme en communicatie in de hulpverlening, module 4: interculturele hulpverlening (Ethnocentrism and communication in care, module 4: intercultural care)*. Utrecht St. Landelijke Federatie Welzijnsorganisaties voor Surinamers (Utrecht Foundation National Federation of Surinamese Welfare Organizations), pp. 171-194.

Jessurun, C.M. (2004), 'Hoe meer verschillen, hoe meer vreugd' ('The more differences, the

merrier'). In: R. Beunderman, A. Savenije, M. Mattheijer en P. Willems (eds.), *Meer kleur in de jeugd-GGZ (More colour in youth mental healthcare)*. Assen: Koninklijke Van Gorcum.
Jessurun, C.M. (2010), *Transculturele vaardigheden voor therapeuten (Transcultural skills for therapists)*. Bussum: Coutinho.
Jong, P. de en I. Berg (2001), 'Co-Constructing Cooperation with Mandated Clients', *Social Work*, 46, pp. 361-375.
Kagitçibasi, C. (1996), *Family and Human development across cultures. A view from the other side.* Mahwah, NJ: Lawrence Erlbaum.
Komter, A. en T. Knijn (2004), 'Zwarte schapen in de familie' ('Black sheep in the family'), *DEMOS*, vol. 20, nr. 10.
Kouratovsky, V. (2008), 'Inwikkeling en het belang van cultuursensitieve diagnostiek en therapie,' ('Envelopment and the importance of culturally sensitive diagnostics and therapy'). In: T.I. Oei en L. Kaiser (eds.), *Forensische psychiatrie onderweg (Forensic psychiatry)*, pp. 371-385. Nijmegen: Wolf Legal Publishers.
Krznaric, R. (2015), *Empathy*. Rider.
Lau, A, (1995), 'Gender; power and relationships, Etno-cultural and religious issues'. In: C. Burk en B. Speed (eds.), *Gender, power and relationships*. London: Routledge.
Levinas, E (English 1969) *Totality and Infinity: An Essay on Exteriority*. Pittsburgh: Duquesne University Press.
Meurs, P. en A. Gailly (1999), *Wortelen in andere aarde, Migrantengezinnen en hulpverleners ontmoeten cultuurverschil (Taking root in different ground, Migrant families and care workers encounter cultural differences)*. Leuven/Amersfoort: Acco.
Norbert, E. (1987), *Die Gesellschaft der Individuen*. Frankfurt a. M.
Perry, B. en M. Szalavitz (2011), *Born for love*. HarperCollins Publishers Inc.
Ramdas, A. (1992), 'Heimwee' ('Homesick'). In: A. Ramdas, *De papegaai, de stier en de klimmende bougainvillea, essays (The parrot, the bull and the climbing bougainvillea)*. De Bezige Bij.
Rhmaty, F. (2011), *Traumaverwerking met vluchtelingen (Trauma processing with refugees)*. Assen: Koninklijke Van Gorcum.
Rijk, R. de, F. Zitman en R. de Kloet (2004), 'Neuro-endocrinologie van de stressrespons' ('Neuroendocrinology of the stress response'). In: J.E. Hovens, A.J.M. Loonen en L. Timmerman (eds.), *Handboek neurobiologische psychiatrie (Manual neurobiological psychiatry)*. De Tijdstroom.
Roth, J. (1996), 'Workshop intercultural concepts 3rd European summer seminar in intercultural studies'.
Schaap, P.M. en E. Meijerink (2004), *De nieuwe veenkoloniën (The new peat colonies)*. Ekkers & Paauw.
Schutte, X., 'Moeder bepaalt je succes' ('Mother is the key to your success'), *de Volkskrant*, 17 September 2005.
Selten, J.P. (2002), 'Epidemiologie van schizofrenie bij migranten in Nederland' ('Epidemiology of schizophrenia among migrants in the Netherlands'), *Tijdschrift voor psychiatrie* 44-10, pp. 665-675.
Shazer, S. de (1991), *Putting difference to work*. New York: Norton.
Somers, S., K. Tjin A Djie en I. Zwaan (2012), 'De therapeut als edelsmid'('The therapist as jeweller'). In: Y. te Poel et al. (ed.), *Interculturele diagnostiek bij kinderen en jongeren (Intercultural diagnostics among children and young people)*. NIP & NVO.
Sterman, D. (1996), *Een olijfboom op de ijsberg. Een transcultureel-psychiatrische visie op en behandeling van jonge Noord-Afrikanen en hun families. (An olive tree on the iceberg. A transcultural-psychiatric vision on and treatment of young North Africans and their families.)* Nederlands Centrum Buitenlanders (Dutch Center for Foreigners); republished by Pharos (2007).
Stoelinga, B. (2001), *Naar een brede professionaliteit. De wensen en behoeften van de klant als uitgangspunt (Towards a broad form of professionalism. The wishes and needs of the client as the starting point)*. Maatwerk 2.
Tavecchio, L. en H. Bos (eds.) (2011), 'Pedagogiek, wetenschappelijk forum voor opvoeding, onderwijs en vorming', *Thema: Vaderschap, rol van vaders in opvoeding van kinderen en diversiteit in vaderschap* ('Pedagogy, scientific forum for parenting, education and training', *Theme: Fatherhood, role of fathers in raising children and diversity in fatherhood*) 31 nr. 1. Van Gorcum.
Tjin A Djie, K. (2000), 'Ouderschap in een wij-systeem' ('Parenthood in a we-system'), Second Alice van der Pas Lecture.
Tjin A Djie, K. (2002), 'De bijzondere opdracht van migrantenkinderen' ('The special assignment of migrant children'). In: C.J.A. Roosen, A. Savenije, A. Kolman en R. Beunderman (eds.) *'Over*

een grens', Psychotherapie met adolescenten ('Across a border', Psychotherapy with adolescents), Assen: Koninklijke Van Gorcum.

Tjin A Djie, K. (2003), 'Beschermjassen, een wijze van hulpverlenen waardoor ouders en kinderen uit wij-systemen worden ingebed in hun familie en cultuur' ('Protective wraps, a way of providing care through which parents and children from we-oriented systems are embedded in their family and cuture'), Systeemtherapie (System Therapy), 15 (1), pp. 17-39.

Tjin A Djie, K. en I. Zwaan (2010), Managen van diversiteit op de werkvloer (Managing diversity at work). Assen: Koninklijke Van Gorcum.

Tjin A Djie, K. en I. Zwaan (2012), 'Beschermjassen als baken voor intercultureel werken, Mobiliseren van de eigen oplossingsstrategieën van familiesystemen' ('Protective wraps as a beacon for intercultural work, Mobilising solution strategies within family systems'). In: M. Berk, K. Verhaar, A. Hoogenboom et al. (eds.), De jeugdprofessional in ontwikkeling (The youth professional in the making). Kluwer.

Tjin A Djie, K. en I. Zwaan (2013), De Familieziel, hoe je geschiedenis je kan helpen op je levenspad (The Family Soul, How your history can help you on your life path). Amsterdam: Prometheus Bert Bakker.

Tjin A Djie, K. en I. Zwaan (2013), 'Beschermjassen: het zelfoplossend vermogen van families' ('Protective Wraps: problem-solving skills within families'), Tijdschrift Kinder- & Jeugdpsychotherapie 40, nr. 4.

Tjin A Djie, K. en I. Zwaan (2015), Beschermjassen op school, aandacht voor verschil in het onderwijs (Protective wraps at school, attention to different aspects in education). Assen: Koninklijke van Gorcum

Tjin A Djie, K. en I. Zwaan (2015), ' Vaderschap in relatie tot familie cultuur en historie' ('Fatherhood in relation to family culture and history'), Tijdschrift Kinder- en Jeugdpsychotherapie, vol. 42, nr. 4.

Turnell, A. en S. Edwards (1999), Signs Of Safety: a solution and safety oriented approach to child protection. New York: WW Norton.

Turner, V.W. (1969), The ritual process: Structure and anti-structure (The ritual process: Structure and anti-structure).

Venema, T. (1992), Famiri Nanga Kulturu, Creoolse sociale verhoudingen en Winti in Amsterdam (Famiri Nanga Kulturu, Creole social relationships and Winti in Amsterdam). Amsterdam: Het Spinhuis.

Waal, F. de (2009), Een tijd voor empathie (The age of empathy). Contact.

Waal, F. de (2013), De Bonobo en de tien geboden (The Bonobo and the atheist). Atlas Contact.

Watzlawick, W., J.H. Beavin en D.D. Jackson (2014). Pragmatics of Human Communication. W.W. Norton & Company Ltd.

Wekker, G. (1998), 'Gender, identiteitsvorming en multiculturalisme: notities over de Nederlandse multiculturele samenleving' ('Gender, shaping identity and multiculturalism: notes on Dutch multicultural society'), In: K. Geuijen (eds.), Multiculturalisme (Multiculturalism). Lemma.

Winnicott, D. (1953), 'Transitional objects and transitional phenomena', Int. J. Psychoanal., 34:89-97.

Worrall, J. (2005), Grandparents Raising Grandchildren: A handbook for grandparents and other kin givers. Grandparents Raising Grandchildren Trust Auckland Boughtwood Printing House.

Zwaan, I. (2013), De afwezige vader bestaat niet, en waarom vaders niet moeten moederen (The absent father does not exist, and why fathers should not try mothering). Amsterdam: Prometheus Bert Bakker.

Zwaan, I. (2016), Sven tot het einde, de complexe praktijk rondom een puber met een LVB, ODD en een levensbedreigende ziekte (Sven until the end, the complex practice around an adolescent suffering from a mild intellectual disability, ODD, and a life threatening disease). Assen: Koninklijke van Gorcum.